Leading from the Edge

Other titles from Bloomsbury Education:

8 Qualities of Successful School Leaders: The Desert Island Challenge by Jeremy Sutcliffe

Creating Tomorrow's Schools Today by Richard Gerver

Getting the Buggers to Behave by Sue Cowley

How to Survive an Ofsted Inspection by Sarah Findlater

Lesson Planning Tweaks for Teachers by Melanie Aberson and Debbie Light

Teacher Toolkit by Ross Morrison McGill

The A-Z of School Improvement by Tim Brighouse and David Woods

Leading from the Edge

A school leader's guide to recognising and overcoming stress

by James Hilton

Foreword by Richard Gerver

BLOOMSBURY

LONDON · OXFORD · NEW YORK · NEW DELHI · SYDNEY

Bloomsbury Education

An imprint of Bloomsbury Publishing Plc

50 Bedford Square	1385 Broadway
London	New York
WC1B 3DP	NY 10018
UK	USA

www.bloomsbury.com

Bloomsbury is a registered trade mark of Bloomsbury Publishing Plc

First published 2016

British Library Cataloguing-in-Publication Data

A catalogue record for this book is available from the British Library.

ISBN:
PB 9781472917348
ePub 9781472917355
ePDF 9781472917362

Library of Congress Cataloging-in-Publication Data

A catalog record for this book is available from the Library of Congress.

10 9 8 7 6 5 4 3 2 1

Typeset by Newgen Knowledge Works (P) Ltd., Chennai, India
Printed by CPI Group (UK) Ltd, Croydon, CR0 4YY

This book is produced using paper that is made from wood grown in managed,
sustainable forests. It is natural, renewable and recyclable. The logging and manufacturing
processes conform to the environmental regulations of the country of origin.

To view more of our titles please visit www.bloomsbury.com

This book is for my Dad – I wish he was here to read it,
but I sensed him watching over my shoulder as it was written.

I would like to thank my family and friends for their loving support
and helping me to believe in myself again. You know who you are.

Contents

Acknowledgements

I would like to thank my fantastic editors at Bloomsbury:

Holly Gardner, for her faith and confidence in a book that I had still yet to write and for shaping it into the product that you now hold in your hands. I am truly grateful! Miriam Davey, for picking up the reigns and doing such a wonderful job of finalising my manuscript and getting it to print!

Thank you too to the remarkable Chris Roome, for his care and guidance when I was a patient and for his much valued advice, input and encouragement during the writing of this book.

I would also like to extend my heartfelt thanks to the many people who have given so generously of their time with their ideas, advice, encouragement and support:

Peter Anderton, David Bateson, Paul Bennett, Dr Paul Birch, Lisa Bird, Peter Blunsdon, Mandy Bryant, Dr John Charlton, Carol Clemens, Clive Clemens, Professor Cary Cooper, Andy Cope, Richard Gerver, Sue Goodall, Charlotte Hilton, Jonathan Hilton, Julia Hilton, Pat Hilton, Rachel Hilton, Bernadette Hunter, Neil Jones, Joy King, Karina Lyburn, Wayne Madsen, Steve Munby, John Rees, Liz Reynolds, Nick Reynolds, Ben Robinson, Sir Ken Robinson, Nikki Roome, Wendy Rose, Jane Rutherford, Tony Seymour, Lynne Skeith, Trevor Skeith, Ava Sturridge-Packer, Mick Taylor, Nicky Taylor, Chris Thinnes, Jann Tucker, Tony Tucker, Pam Underwood, Ash Venkatesh, and Chris Wheatley.

Foreword – Who cares?

The summer of 1997 was a momentous one; a new UK government swept to power on a feel-good wave of 'things can only get better'. It was time for 'Cool Britannia'. Amidst the excitement, I had a moment of my own; a moment that would literally change my life forever. After over a year of application after application and endless knockbacks, I was appointed as a deputy headteacher. It was one of those snapshot moments when you get a jolt of positivity that shoots through you and generates immense energy and optimism. It was an intoxicating summer.

That was when I first remember meeting James Hilton, over the interview table. He was the recently confirmed permanent head of a large primary school in Derbyshire looking for a new deputy and I was about to be appointed to fill that role. He was young to be a headteacher and very young to be the head of such a large primary school with 500 pupils on roll. He was dynamic and fresh; one of the first of the new breed of headteacher who had to operate far more like the CEO of a midsize business. He was an instinctive and measured risk-taker; he appointed me as his deputy after all, when I had only been teaching for five years.

We worked together for three years. They were, without a doubt, three of the most exciting, challenging and rewarding years of my career. The greatest gift for me was a lasting friendship that holds strong today.

I learnt so much from James, particularly from his humanity and unshakeable belief in the development of people rather than structures and his total focus on the rights of the children in our care. Our relationship was one of those rare occurrences; the chemistry of two professionals who just worked brilliantly together with genuine trust and respect. As a leader, James was courageous and would inspire others to take the lead or the spotlight and to evolve; empowerment not control.

That kind of leadership takes a huge sense of character and can take its toll both emotionally and physically.

During our three years of working together, I saw him at times struggle with his burden but never sacrifice his beliefs. In hindsight, it is clear that he was suffering from the early signs of work-related stress. I saw him try to hide his emerging illness given the still prevalent belief that stress was a sign of weakness – of a fragile mind and body. I saw, first hand, the impact it had on his decision-making and relationships.

Ultimately, over many years of what became a life-threatening struggle, I saw him win through. Even at the darkest moments, James never lost his courage or selfless focus on others. At times though this didn't help him, as he never gave himself the space, time or permission to reflect on his own welfare.

What made James an outstanding teacher and headteacher was his ability and desire to learn. Since leaving the high-pressure world of headship, he has had the time and space to reflect on and research his own journey which has led to this remarkable book.

When James asked me if I would be prepared to write this foreword, I was honoured. When you start reading, you will immediately discover the honesty, insight and courage which makes this book so powerful and authentic. It is much like the man himself.

Leading from the Edge, could not be timelier. In my opinion, stress is the most significant and yet most misunderstood illness of the 21st century. It is certainly one of the greatest barriers to the development and radical change our education system truly needs if we are to create a system worthy of our children and that can ensure that they thrive in their increasingly complex future.

There is an irony to all of this, I think, because our education system is not designed to help us develop the skills, attributes and behaviours that aid us to cope with uncertainty, and I believe that it is one of the key reasons that we are seeing such a dramatic rise in stress-related illness, especially amongst our young.

One of the routes into stress is the growing belief that we have less and less control over our problems, over our decisions and over our lives. We tend to become less proactive and more reactive. Our instinct is to hunker down, to isolate and to hope that the storm passes. This book is part of the antidote.

We must take control of this illness by recognising it, understanding it and acting against it. We must do more to help ourselves and others if we are to hope to triumph as a society.

The more people I meet and the more places I travel, the more I am aware of the impact of stress on people's personal and professional lives. That same government that swept to power in 1997, had at its heart one of the first high-profile figures to admit suffering from a stress-related illness – Alastair Campbell. It was a government that ultimately imploded because it went from functioning proactively to reactively, leading to people losing faith and trust in its leadership.

As teachers, we are all leaders. In my opinion, teaching is the greatest job in the world, and to be a headteacher is the pinnacle of that profession. It is a job where our role is to promote hope, aspiration and value. It is more than a job actually, it is a vocation; teachers are role models not just for children but for future society and as such we should take the lead in the fight to minimise the impact of stress on our ability to create brighter futures for ourselves.

James Hilton changed my life once before and this book has the potential to do so again; thank you James, let the fight back begin!

Richard Gerver

Speaker, author and broadcaster

Introduction

In May 2012, Sir Michael Wilshaw, the head of Ofsted, told a conference of headteachers that headteachers do not know what stress is.

'Stress is what my father felt, who struggled to find a job in the 50s and 60s and who often had to work long hours in three different jobs and at weekends to support a growing family.'

This book seeks to expose and deconstruct the myth that stress does not, and cannot, exist in modern educational leadership.

The pressures have been building for a while. Most people have higher imposed targets than ever before, yet fewer people to help to achieve them. The result is that most people are working harder for longer. There is an increasing sense of disenfranchisement, with school leaders experiencing a far higher degree of accountability set against a background of a decreasing sense of empowerment.

Despite the mounting pressures of the modern workplace, 'stress' is not only commonly misunderstood but has gone and got itself a bad name.

Stress is not the only pressure facing school leaders and the challenge is not only to recognise and manage stress in themselves, but in the people they lead. It is the single most significant barrier to school improvement, as well as to successful and sustainable educational leadership.

Being a school leader is the greatest job in the world – an opportunity to help shape the next generation. Many school leaders experience stress as a result of a feeling of powerlessness in an education system characterised by exponential change. Few feel able to talk about it openly for fear of being judged, leading to a sense of isolation. **Stress is the elephant in the room**.

As an experienced primary head, in my second headship, I had a nervous breakdown in 2006/7 brought on by work-related stress. After a significant period of absence, I returned to headship, more self-aware than before and determined to try and look at life differently. I was fortunate to be referred to Chris Roome, a mental health therapist, who taught me many of the positive strategies that I learned in my recovery.

After several more successful years in headship, I finally left in 2013. I now work as a speaker and trainer with a wide variety of clients including the National Association of Head Teachers (NAHT), schools, universities, businesses, the National Health Service (NHS), local government and charities. Time and space has given me the opportunity to look back and reflect on my battles with stress and what I have learned from them.

I share my leadership story in the hope that it will help others. Having recently had the honour of giving the opening keynote speech at the NAHT annual conference, I know from the feedback I have received, that aspects of my experiences will resonate with many people. For others, I hope that it will help them to recognise the symptoms of stress in colleagues and enable them to support them.

This is not intended to be an academic textbook. Nor is it a medical journal. This book is a practical, honest, provocative and, occasionally, humorous account of the challenges of leading a 21st century school. It is filled with scenarios and related coping strategies that will I hope inspire, encourage and reassure. It is an authentic, intelligent and powerful reflection on the challenges faced by those wanting to transform the lives of a school, its community and its children.

As well as sharing some of my own stories and learning, the book contains interviews with leaders in education from a wide variety of contexts who have generously shared their perspectives and advice on managing personal stress as well as that of the colleagues they have lead.

Also contained within these pages is the collective wisdom gathered from Chris and other professionals that will allow you to take back control over some of the most common manifestations of stress.

If this book helps shines a light and encourage debate on an issue that has lurked in the dark for too long then that is good. If it helps other people experiencing stress to realise that they are not alone, then that is better. If it encourages people to have conversations they have never had before, both at a school and national level, then that would be the best of all.

Chris Roome

I am delighted that Chris Roome has acted as a consultant in the writing of this book. He has taught me many stress management techniques over the years and he is quoted and offers wisdom throughout the following pages.

Chris Roome is a registered mental nurse (RMN) with over forty years of experience working in psychiatry in Derbyshire.

He has developed services locally relating to the transition from hospital to community care. As team leader of the community mental health team he was passionate about clinical excellence and integrated community services.

Chris believes that everyone should have a voice and be listened to; everybody has the capacity to change and discover their potential. He has worked for a busy inner-city GP surgery for the past fifteen years seeing people with a wide range of psychological difficulties.

Away from work Chris embraces country living. He is a married man with four children and four grandchildren. Hobbies include gardening and golf and he is a diehard fan of Derby County.

For printable versions of the Challenges in the book, please visit: www.bloomsbury. com/hilton-leading-from-the-edge

1 A long way down – My story

You can't fall if you don't climb. But there's no joy in living your whole life on the ground.

Unknown

A (very!) brief history of time

As a child I climbed anything – the climbing frame in my garden, trees and rocks in the nearby woods . . . (I cannot think the Health and Safety Executive (HSE) existed back then, otherwise we would have been climbing in bubble wrap!) As a large family, the cost of foreign travel was quite prohibitive and actually fairly unusual back then. We regularly holidayed in Woolacombe Bay in Devon. Just below where we stayed was a small, enclosed and beautifully sandy beach. As the youngest of five children I spent many a happy hour there being buried up to my head in sand by my elder siblings, unable to move. (They also used to tie me to a swing at the end of our garden. They were playing weren't they?) Over the years I regularly shimmied up a 45 degree rock face from the beach to the cliff top without fear. And then in 1970 something changed. An RAF search and rescue helicopter was coming in to land on the cliff top having rescued some fisherman caught out by the advancing tide. I started climbing the rock face desperate to watch the yellow Sea King helicopter land. Half way up, I made the mistake of turning round and looking down at the beach. It suddenly seemed such a long way down and although I knew where I wanted to get to, the safety of the cliff top seemed so very far away. I did not shout or cry, I just froze completely unable to move up or down. I can remember my dad clambering up to rescue me, talking me through move by move what I needed to do with my hands and feet in order to reach a place of safety.

In 2006, I was twenty years into my teaching career and in the third year of my second primary school headship and this was to prove the most eventful year so far.

Over the preceding years, I had been seconded by the Local Education Authority (LEA) on several occasions to support a range of projects including acting head of a school deemed by Ofsted to have 'serious weaknesses'. I would like to think that I was well thought of. My first headship had been of one of the largest primary schools in the county, in an ex-mining community. I had spent eight very happy years there as a deputy working for Pam Underwood, a head who I admired greatly and who had taken a real chance on me as I had only had four years teaching experience at that point. When she came to retire, I was encouraged to apply for the position and was successful. I was able to appoint a young, keen and talented deputy head, Richard Gerver, and I had five successful years as head. Having worked there as a deputy for so long and having enjoyed good working relationships; people were willing me to do well.

However, after thirteen years at the school, I knew that if I did not move soon, I would probably stay forever, which I was not convinced would be the best thing for me, nor indeed the school.

I found myself in a salary trap. With a young family that was settled and children at school, we did not want to relocate and with my first headship already being of a large school there were comparatively few positions that I could apply for without taking a drop in salary. And then the position of headteacher came up at the largest primary school in the county. This one was certainly worth applying for. The school already had 500 pupils on roll and a local housing boom meant that it was expected to grow by a further 150 pupils. As it turned out, it was to become one of the largest primary schools in the country, with over 800 pupils. It was mostly a new build. I remember visiting and being blown away by the light, airy feel of the classrooms and the beautiful displays. It even had pitched roofs! No more buckets every time the heavens opened. There were even plans on the table to build a second hall and new kitchens.

There was a high level of interest in the position as the size of the school ensured that the salary would be attractive to a lot of people. I was thrilled to get an interview alongside a couple of heads who I knew and had enormous respect for as well as several candidates from further afield. I was on cloud nine when, after a gruelling two-day selection process and much nervous pacing, they offered me the position.

My first couple of years were a bumpy ride. As pupil numbers grew rapidly, it took time for funding to catch up. This would have been all right if the following year pupil numbers had stabilised, but they continued to grow. We would often gain as many as thirty pupils mid-year and of course they never came in a nice even spread across the year groups. As a result, this funding 'catch-up' phenomenon would repeat itself year on year resulting in a significant deficit budget situation. I was fortunate to have a really supportive governing body and together we took some tough but necessary staffing decisions that inevitably dented morale. I was aware that the staff did not really know me at this point and that I could not assume the loyalty that I had carried over when I moved from being deputy to head in my previous school. That loyalty had to be earned and rightly so. It somehow felt a lonelier position to be in.

We appointed a deputy head internally and externally a Foundation Stage co-ordinator, Wendy Rose, who was blessed with great people skills, was an outstanding teacher and full of great ideas. Things were on the up and morale began to improve again. This was cemented by retaining a judgement of 'Good' in the next Ofsted inspection. Pupil numbers continued to rise, buildings continued to appear in order to provide the classrooms and facilities needed to cater for the extra numbers (in fact, it seemed builders were rarely off the site). Pupil outcomes remained high and there were even plans to rebuild the school's dilapidated swimming pool that had first been built in the 1970s. A popular selling point of the school, it was nonetheless terribly expensive to heat and a nightmare to maintain. With a really dynamic Parent Teachers and Friends Association (PTFA) combining forces with the local Rotary club, plans were well on their way to raise the money to secure the use of the pool for the next generation.

So, things were certainly looking up in 2006 with much to celebrate and to look forward to.

Surely there could be no connection between back pains I had been getting on and off and my work situation? They were only muscular pains after all. I just wasn't terribly good at remembering to do the exercises that the osteopath, that I had started seeing, had given me. If I had kept a diary back then, I might have noted that the migraines that I had occasionally been having over the last couple of years, were becoming more frequent. But, I was just tired and very, very busy.

There seemed to be a huge number of evening meetings and events at school, which I really didn't mind because I got on really well with the governing body and the members of the PTFA. Meetings and events did not seem like a chore.

However, I was struggling to fit in rehearsals for the amateur dramatics productions that I had loved so much. Leading up to a performance, we would usually rehearse twice a week and technical and dress rehearsals took up the whole of the weekend before the run. If I managed to plan my evening meetings at school around the rehearsals then I could be out every night of the week, which was unfair on my family and left me exhausted. Alternatively, if I missed some rehearsals, I felt under-rehearsed. But it wasn't just the time rehearsing, it was the time spent learning the lines. When I was at university I could pick up a pretty decent approximation of the lines on the page after running a scene a couple of times. As I got older that skill deserted me, and the trail of masking tape around the set with 'bogey lines' that I just could not remember, grew longer and longer. I even started having the classic actor's nightmare of dreaming I was on stage in a play but having no idea which play it was!

I came up with a solution. At first, I just stopped performing on stage and worked behind the scenes as stage manager. I missed the buzz of making the audience laugh in bedroom farces and the recognition in reviews, but at least I didn't need to learn lines. Ultimately, I gave up altogether and the group disbanded sometime later. I would wish to stress that this was not as a result of my departure from the stage but more to do with our brilliant and award-winning director suffering ill health.

I now had no hobby and few interests outside of work.

For some reason I was also beginning to feel a tightness in my chest and shortness of breath on my way to work. It was nothing to do with the back pain and migraines, of course!

At the bottom of my garden is an enormous sycamore tree. It is not that we have a particularly large garden I would hasten to add! The tree is actually planted in the pub behind us. It predates the house and overhangs our property. Every year, the sycamore seeds fall on our lawn. I watch the first few fall gently spinning like the helicopters we imagined they were back when I was at primary school. They are things of beauty and they motivate me to spend time in the garden (I am not a natural gardener!), both clearing them up and tending to other jobs that need doing. As the days go by, more fall and I hasten into the garden to sweep them up and keep the lawn vaguely green in colour.

The seeds continue to fall, and despite my attempts to resist the slow, but steady aerial bombardment, the lawn is now covered in a thick carpet of seeds, with little green in sight.

I feel swamped – not knowing where to begin.

By spring 2006, I had stopped attending the LEA area heads meetings, which mostly seemed full of doom and gloom. I had also stopped going to the local cluster headteachers' meetings. They were a really good group of people but I always came away feeling that my to do list (which I rarely seemed to make any impact on anyway), had just got longer. I now know that it was just my perception and that we were all, as individuals, slightly more on top of some things than others. We just kept quiet on those topics we weren't on top of! Anyway, I didn't have the time to go to meetings, budget issues were ever present and with well over 75 members of staff by this stage, we seemed to be forever interviewing or trying to find a creative solution to the latest promotion, maternity leave, long-term absence or secondment. With an ever expanding site, increasing numbers of classes and five playgrounds, I was struggling to get round the school grounds, yet alone stay on top of the paperwork or be accessible to all the parents who wanted appointments to see me.

I did not seem to be able to hold down my breakfast in the mornings and had started to develop a gagging reflex to cleaning my teeth, although strangely not when I brushed them at night. It was easier to not eat breakfast and instead drink copious cups of coffee when I arrived at work.

And anyway the gagging reflex was not connected to the back pain, migraines and shortness of breath.

In the autumn term, you could add into the mix of ingredients the behavioural issues at different ends of the school. At this stage I was the only senior member of staff off timetable for much of the time and so was often called on for backup. Other work just seemed to pile up. It must have been becoming clear to other people that something was amiss as I became increasingly aware of other members of the Senior Leadership Team (SLT) being called on to deal with issues with pupils and parents instead of me, even if that meant them coming out of class.

Perhaps it was the gaunt and hollow-eyed look of someone who can rarely sleep, or perhaps it was the stammer I had developed which had now become quite pronounced when I spoke to large groups of people, or when dealing with angry parents or other stressful situations?

I was not certain, but these were surely not connected with the back pain, migraines, shortness of breath and gagging that I had been experiencing... Or were they?

By autumn half-term 2006, I could barely drive myself to work. There was a roundabout almost exactly halfway between home and school. On one cold November morning, I reached the roundabout and could go no further. I had to pull over. I had severe chest pains, a wave of nausea and I had broken out in an icy, cold sweat. I thought my number was up, fearing that I was having a heart attack. The sensation eventually passed sufficiently for me to make it into work, if somewhat late. Unfortunately this pattern of events repeated itself several times more over the coming weeks with the same overwhelming sense of panic and severe pain and nausea at exactly the same roundabout, halfway between home and school. It was never an issue on the return journey.

With the Christmas season now firmly upon us, there were multiple carol concerts and nativity performances, at which the head traditionally welcomed parents and thanked the children at the end. I could manage neither as I was terrified of stammering. Our Foundation Stage team leader and Deputy Head covered many of these duties. I even had to bow out of organising the junior trip to the local Christmas pantomime, something that, with my amateur dramatic connections, I normally thoroughly enjoyed. I became increasingly tearful.

The stammering had spilled over into home life and I have to say I was not very tolerant at home, and did not want to socialise. I was short-tempered and morose. It was not the best of Christmas holidays. I don't think I even tasted the turkey on Christmas Day. I barely slept, but when I did, I would dream of school and catastrophise the worst possible outcomes to the many situations or problems that were troubling me.

I returned to school in January 2007, but whatever brief respite the Christmas break had offered soon dissipated and so I threw myself (not literally) into the swimming pool project. After a massive fundraising drive, construction work on the new building was nearing completion and a grand opening, with many local VIPs, was being planned for the end of the month. There was great excitement and even a Commonwealth medallist in swimming due to cut the ribbon. I spent quite a bit of time over at the pool that month, watching things come together as construction workers raced against the clock to complete the project in time for the grand opening. The atmosphere was similar to that which we see on TV programmes like *DIY SOS – the big build* – Would we make it on time? Of course we did – deadlines focus the mind brilliantly! I experienced a huge sense of satisfaction in seeing the project to its conclusion. The opening ceremony was a great success, with the many guests suitably impressed with the clean lines of the new building and the magnitude of what had been achieved. I went home happier than I had been in some months.

Monday morning arrived and I got up and took the dog for a walk, as I did every day before school. As I walked, I became aware of a twinge in my lower back. This was nothing new and so I ignored it, but by the time I had returned to the house, it had worsened. Half an hour before I was due to go to work, I began to experience spasms of searing pain in my lower back. It was excruciating and came in waves approximately every three minutes. As this pattern of timing emerged, I found myself tensing after a couple of minutes anticipating the next wave of pain. Now I know I am prone to be dramatic and I am prone to 'man flu' (I don't get a cold very often, but when I do, everyone knows about it!) but I think this was probably the closest I will get to experiencing the pain of childbirth, although without the joy and exhilaration that comes at the end of the process.

I was lying on the lounge floor by this stage and I am not ashamed to say that I was crying. There was talk about going to the doctors but every time I tried to move it set a new spasm in motion. Calling an ambulance seemed an overreaction to what was essentially muscular discomfort and so Rachel, my wife, called the NHS Direct Helpline who advised putting frozen peas in a tea towel under my back to help to relax the muscles. We had some strong(ish) painkillers in the medicine cabinet, and so I took a sensible dose of these. My wife rang school and told them that I would not be in. Sleep eventually overtook me. I remained flat on the lounge floor day and night for several days.

I spent many days during my childhood with my family playing in Bradgate Park in Leicestershire. If I were to take you for a walk there and abandon you when the bracken was at its highest, the chances are quite high that unless you have a very well-defined sense of direction, you would get lost. (I have no sense of direction at all – unless my journey involves either the M1 or A38, I stand no chance without a satnav). There are so many paths that criss-cross the park that it is very difficult to see where and how they join up from ground level if you have not been there before. However, if I were to take you up 100 feet into the skies above Bradgate Park in a hot-air balloon, you would not only see the deer roaming free, the ruins of Lady Jane Grey's house (Queen of England for just nine days before she was executed) and many other beautiful landscape features, you would see all the paths and exactly where and how they all join up. With perspective, gained with distance, you would understand the connectivity, and when brought safely back down amongst the bracken-lined paths you would be able to determine your route forward.

You, as the reader, have hovered over my situation in 2006 and early 2007 as if in a hot-air balloon, watching events unfold with a perspective that I was not afforded, or at least I had lost, at ground level. You will have seen the warning signs that I had ignored.

As with the paths at Bradgate Park, I had truly lost all sense of how things were connected. You will have guessed, I am sure, pretty early on in events that the back pain, increasing number of migraines, shortness of breath, chest pains, lack of sleep, lack of appetite and short temper were indeed all connected. They were all manifestations of a mind and body that had spent too much time in 'fight or flight' mode. When warning lights come on in your car, they are there to advise you to take action, to both protect the car and keep you safe. Ignoring a single light for too long can be a risky strategy (you can ignore the fuel warning light for a few miles but sooner or later you will grind to a halt), but when your whole instrument panel is lit up like a Christmas tree, there is, most probably, a significant underlying problem and you would be well advised to contact your local garage. Ploughing on regardless is not to be recommended – particularly as a long-term strategy.

In February 2006, my engine had seized up completely. I was once again that boy frozen on the rock face unable to move up or down. I had my foot on the accelerator and the brake at the same time.

I was suffering, as is common in cases of work-related stress, from a mixture of anxiety and depression.

What are the recognised symptoms of stress?

Chris says . . .

There are many possible indicators of stress and not everyone will exhibit them all. Symptoms will often include a number of the following:

- **Sleep** – problems in either falling, or remaining asleep.
- **Appetite** – a tendency to comfort eat (or drink), or a loss of appetite.

- **Mood** – tearfulness, lack of motivation either at work and or home (e.g. not cleaning the house, or paying no attention to your physical appearance).
- **Concentration** – unable to settle to tasks, or a tendency to have to read a page in a book several times over.
- **Tolerance** – uncharacteristic road rage, screaming at the kids, or avoidance strategies such as staying in bed.
- **Libido** – loss of sex drive.

Challenge: simple stress test

If you think you might be suffering from work-related stress, try scoring yourself on this simple test. For each question, think about how many times you have experienced the sympton described during the last month and score yourself using the following scale:

0 = Never   1 = Sometimes   2 = Often   3 = Very often

SECTION	QUESTION		SCORE
A	1	Twitching or facial tics	
	2	Headaches or migraines	
	3	Shoulder or back pain	
	4	Nausea	
	5	Pounding heart	
	6	Tightness of the chest	
	7	Stomach upsets	
	8	Tearfulness	
	9	Excessive perspiration other than during exercise	
	10	Colds	
		Section A total score (out of possible 30)	
B	1	Tiredness or lack of energy	
	2	Difficulty getting to sleep or remaining asleep	
	3	Difficulty concentrating on tasks or retaining information	
	4	Getting little pleasure from doing things, or having no interest in own appearance	
	5	Overeating or under-eating	

	6	Fidgeting or lacking motivation to move (e.g. getting out of bed)	
	7	Feeling down or lacking hope	
	8	Feeling a sense of failure or that you have let others down (at home or at work)	
	9	Thinking that other people would be better off without you	
		Section B total score (out of possible 27)	
C	1	Easily annoyed and irritable	
	2	Have difficulty relaxing	
	3	Very restless, unable to settle to anything or keep still	
	4	Worrying a lot about a wide range of issues	
	5	Unable to control high levels of worrying	
	6	Feeling nervous or on edge	
	7	Sense of foreboding – anxious that something terrible is about to happen	
		Section C total score (out of possible 21)	
		Total score (out of a possible 78)	

Results – How did you get on?

I have retrospectively filled in this form considering my physical and mental health in late 2006/early 2007. You will probably realise given my account earlier in the chapter that I 'ticked many of the boxes' and so would score fairly highly on this. For comparison purposes, I would have scored as follows:

Section A: 17 (out of 30)
Section B: 20 (out of 27)
Section C: 21 (out of 21)
Total score: 58 (out of 78)

Section A: deals with some of the physical manifestations of stress

As you can see, my responses are middle of the range but certainly significant enough for me to have paid my GP a visit (which I didn't). Any one of these symptoms on its own or combined with others could be an indication of stress, but also of other health-related issues – it's always worth getting them checked out (says 'Mr Wise after the event'!)

Section B: looks to explore issues around depression

I scored fairly highly here. I certainly lost interest in doing things and found little to laugh at and enjoy. I had poor concentration levels and even now my memory is not great (ask anyone who knows me!). There were times when I felt a sense of hopelessness and I could not see a way forward. Thankfully I never reached a point where I seriously considered doing any harm to myself.

Section C: explores anxiety levels

Here I scored a majestic 21 out of a possible 21! (As we have established previously I was not particularly academic as a child and to get full marks in a test was something I always aspired to – just not this particular test.)

© James Hilton, 2016

Conclusions

My answers would indicate that I was experiencing some quite significant physical manifestations of stress. Whilst I was certainly suffering from depression, the more significant factor was my level of anxiety, which was through the roof and fed my physical symptoms.

Chris and I have been reviewing what happened some years on for the purposes of this book. It has been a strange but fascinating process for me because I now understand it from his empathetic perspective, tempered with an outside view and clinical understanding of stress, anxiety and depression. He has recently said something to me that has resonated with me at a very deep level. Chris told me that one of his deepest concerns was my stammer, because to have authority with parents and staff I needed to appear confident. It is very difficult to appear confident and authoritative when you are stammering.

I watched a repeat of Channel 4's *Educating Yorkshire* recently. 'Mushy' Musharaf, the young lad struggling to express himself with a stammer, both moved and inspired me in equal measure. If ever there was a positive advertisement for the teaching profession, that programme was it.

One of my all-time favourite films is *Apollo 13*, starring the amazingly talented Tom Hanks. One of the things that I particularly enjoy about it, is that I can allow myself to be sucked in to all the drama and peril of this compelling, true story of a doomed space mission, safe in the existing knowledge that they all make it back home to Earth safely.

The period 2006–7 was, for me, without doubt my lowest ebb. I want to offer you, the reader, the same assurance, that ultimately I 'made it back safely', more self-aware and possibly a little wiser.

Take control . . .

Anxiety and panic

You will see from the interviews that come at the end of every chapter in this book that we all get stressed at work, sometimes. But when the daily stressors at work cause you to feel preoccupied, scared or panicky, then it is time to act. Feeling anxious about work is a learned response to stress. We don't start out in life that way, so it is important to give ourselves space to reflect on what is worrying us and gain some perspective.

- It is very hard to think objectively when you're experiencing fear or anxiety brought on by a stress response. You need to take time out so that you can physically calm down. Take a walk or make a cup of tea.
- Try visualising yourself in a place of calm and tranquillity where you feel safe. What do you see, hear and smell there?
- Define your anxieties. Write them down and be specific – avoiding lumping different things together.
- Find perspective. Without catastrophising and thinking that the worst will *certainly* happen, consider the worst thing that *could* happen. Gain some perspective, e.g. ask yourself: is it life threatening? Am I going to lose my job over this?
- There is much wisdom in the old saying, 'A problem shared is a problem halved'. Talk to a trusted supporter and gain their perspective.
- Expose yourself to your anxiety. Avoidance will only make your anxiety build over time. The more times you expose yourself to your anxiety, the easier it will be to cope with.
- Reward yourself with a treat when you have faced a situation you have been anxious about.
- Remember, you often don't need to face things alone.
- Control the controllable in the situation.
- Whilst elements of the situation may be unpredictable, remind yourself that you *do* have control of how you choose to respond.
- Anticipation is often worse than the reality. Remind yourself of all the times when things worked out better than you expected.
- Be kind to yourself. You don't have to be perfect. Unrealistic self-expectations are likely to cause you to be anxious.
- Accept that you will have bad days, but that a bad day does not mean you have to have a bad week.

- Often, the worst that can happen is a panic attack – not comfortable, by any means, but it will pass.
- If you start to experience a faster heartbeat, tightness of the chest or sweaty palms, stay where you are and simply feel the panic without trying to fight it. See it as a strong wave that will pass and dissipate when it breaks on the shore. It may take up to an hour, but eventually the panic will go. Place the palm of your hand on your stomach and breathe slowly and deeply. Concentrate on breathing from the diaphragm (See Take control – Breathing (see page 28))
- The aim here is to get our minds to cope with panic. Having strategies to cope with anxiety helps to take away the fear of fear.
- Remember, courage is not the absence of fear, but taking action in spite of fear.

Leadership interview

Dr Peter Blunsdon – Former Headteacher, St. John's C.E. Primary School, Belper, Derbyshire

Background

Peter Blunsdon was a primary headteacher 1989 to 2014 St. John's was his second headship (his first was a small village primary) and he has was in post there for 22 years. The school is located in a former mill town and at the time of interview, had 484 pupils on roll.

Stressors

For Peter there are three main stressors associated with the role of headteacher of a large primary school.

1   Firstly, there are the pressures associated with managing long-term staff absence.

    'You simply have no control over it. Parents will ring you and say: "I know you cannot tell me much and I don't want to pry, but can you tell me when they will be coming back?". You can't, because you can't predict it and you often cannot be completely honest with them because of the delicate nature of the situation.'

2   The second significant stressor is competing deadlines. It is a demanding job and, with the many competing calls upon a head's time, it is almost inevitable that you will miss a deadline from time to time and that is not a comfortable feeling.

3   Peter's biggest source of pressure was public accountability.

    'If things are not going very well for any reason it is often very public and quick to be seized upon by parents and the media. There is a tendency to reflect more on failures and disappointments than on successes.'

For Peter, it was not so much the fear of an Ofsted inspection itself but the potential fallout, public humiliation and damage to a school's reputation that can result.

'It is very difficult at times to develop the school you want whilst meeting the national agenda.'

Peter feels that one of the strengths of his school was that they strived to develop the whole child through extensive programmes of residential visits, music, drama and sport. However, he feels that not enough value is placed upon these by those that seek to evaluate and judge our schools.

> 'There is a tension between the emphasis placed upon English and maths and the wider experience and development of a child.'

Coping strategies

Peter feels that part of his longevity in the role of headteacher was down to the fact that he did find it relatively easy to switch off from school. He had a number of strategies to help him unwind:

- avoiding educational programmes on TV
- taking his dog for long walks
- listening to music, watching films and, increasingly, reading stories
- foreign travel.

Managing stress in others

> 'Getting to know your staff is so important.'

Having been at the school for over twenty years with an established staff led to some lengthy professional relationships which Peter says was key in allowing people to feel that they can talk through any worries or difficulties they are experiencing.

> 'You also have to be honest with them. Everyone understands that if someone is off ill there is a knock-on effect on other people and a cost to the school. I also tried to remind people how lucky they are. We are fortunate with holidays, and there are not many jobs where you can find something to laugh about each day. Sometimes you need to raise your head above the battlements and think, "OK, it's been a bad day, but has anybody actually died?"' (Peter's wife is a nurse and often reminds him that when they have a bad day at work, people actually do die).

Advice to new headteachers or other senior leaders

1 Don't be tempted to become a head too early – there's no going back and you could be in there a long time. Take your time and choose carefully.
2 Keep a sense of humour.

3 Have the confidence to know that there *are* some things you can ignore.

4 Take the time to build relationships, particularly with parents. They need to trust you and that trust pays dividends if, and when, you ever have to make a difficult phone call to them.

Summary: Chapter 1

- Stress is no respecter of position, experience or length of service.
- Whilst change can be a good thing stimulating us to develop, rapid change, particularly without a compelling vision, can lead to stress.
- Indicators of stress include difficulties with sleep, appetite, mood, concentration, tolerance and libido.
- Stress can manifest itself in physical symptoms, depression and anxiety, or often a combination of all three.
- We need perspective to realistically review our condition. This can come with distance or from the feedback of trusted colleagues or friends.

2 Stress? What stress? – Facts and stats

I promise you nothing is as chaotic as it seems. Nothing is worth diminishing your health. Nothing is worth poisoning yourself into stress, anxiety, and fear.

Steve Maraboli

Work-related stress is a huge and growing issue in the UK, not only in teaching but in many other walks of life too. So having described to you the onset of my illness in 2006–2007, let us examine some of the very cheery and uplifting statistics, in order to understand the scale of the problem that characterises this often taboo subject.

The figures make compelling reading (at least for those who like reading statistics). Recognising that not everyone will want to pore over my pet interest, I am reminded of the *Choose your own adventure* books I used to read as a child. For those unfamiliar with this now largely defunct literary art form, these books were a crude precursor to games consoles. You could, for example, determine the fate of the central character by choosing from a choice of options:

- Remain on the space station and fight the alien **(turn to p73)** or
- Run to the escape capsule and live to fight another day **(turn to p86).**

So in the spirit of my childhood adventures you can either remain with me here on page 22 and look at some of the statistics around work-related stress **or** you can just take my word for it that it really is a huge issue and go straight to the chapter summary on page 32.

OK – have they gone? Right, gather round stats lovers and let's take a look.

A good starting point to understand the extent of the issue is *Stress-Related and Psychological Disorders in Great Britain 2014* published by the Health and Safety Executive (HSE). This in turn is largely based on a Labour Force Survey (LFS) by the Office of National Statistics (ONS). It's a long report so here are the highlights (or should that be lowlights?):

- *The total number of cases of work-related stress, depression or anxiety in 2013/14 equates to 39% of all work-related illnesses.*
- *Based on the LFS, the estimated cases of work-related stress, depression and anxiety, both new and total cases, have remained broadly flat for more than a decade.*
- *The total number of working days lost due to work-related stress, depression or anxiety was 11.3 million in 2013/14.*
- *The occupations that reported the highest prevalence rates of work-related stress (three-year average) were health professionals (in particular nurses), teaching and educational professionals and public administration and defence.*
- *The main reasons given by respondents as causing their work-related stress were work load pressure, interpersonal relationships (including difficulties with superiors), work-related violence and bullying, changes at work including reduction of resources or staff and additional responsibilities.*

Work-related stress by occupation

The occupations with the highest estimated prevalence rate of work-related stress in GB, averaged over the three years (2010/11, 2011/12 and 2013/14) were as follows:

- *Welfare and housing associate professionals with **2,830 cases** per 100 000 people.*
- *Nurses with **2,630 cases** per 100 000 people.*
- *Teaching and other education professionals with **2,310 cases** per 100 000 people.*
- *Administrative occupations, government and related organisations with **2,310 cases** per 100 000 people.*

These occupations have statistically significantly higher estimated prevalence rates than across all other occupations averaged over the last three-year period.

Age and gender distribution

- *Females have a statistically significantly higher estimated incidence rate of work-related stress than males in 2013/14 with 128,000 female cases as against 115,000 male cases in 2013/14.*
- *The latest available three year average data from GPs suggests the age grouping of 45–54 in both males and females as representing the greatest percentage of cases of work-related mental ill health.*

Country and region of residence

At the time of writing, there are currently no statistically significant differences in prevalence rates of work-related stress when comparing Wales and Scotland to the average across England.

Causes of stress

The main causes of work-related stress reported by general practitioners participating in the THOR-GP reporting scheme between 2011–13 were:

1 *Factors intrinsic to the job*
2 *Interpersonal relationships*
3 *Changes at work*
4 *Professional development*
5 *Home/work interface*

Working days lost

- *Work-related stress caused workers in Great Britain to lose **11.3 million working days** in 2013/14.*
- ***Male workers** accounted for an estimated **5.4 million** days off work.*
- ***Female workers** accounted for an estimated **5.9 million**.*
- *This represents an overall decrease in annual working days lost since 2001/02, when it was 12.9 million days in total. **
- *On average, each person suffering from this work-related stress takes 23 days off work. This is one of the highest average days lost per case figure amongst the health complaints covered in the LFS.*

*This does rather beg the question that, as these figures only represented *reported* cases, is the mental health of the nation actually improving? More likely, in my personal opinion, is that people are more fearful of taking time off, in tough economic times when job security is low and short-term contracts are becoming prevalent. Whilst teaching is undoubtedly a stressful profession, job security remains better than in many other sectors.

In February, 2012, a study by researchers at the University of Nottingham and University of Ulster, was published in the scientific journal *Occupational Medicine*. The study covered tens of thousands of civil servants in Northern Ireland and revealed that employee absence that was due to work-related stress increased significantly during tough economic times.

According to Jonathan Houdmont, the study's lead author:

'The findings suggest that those organisations which seek to reduce work-related stress during austere economic times are likely to experience lower staff absence and greater productivity.'

(J. Houdmont, R. Kerr and K. Addley, 2012)

Increased incidence of dispensation of anti-depressant drugs

The latest report *Prescriptions Dispensed in the Community England 2004–14: (2015)* produced by the Health and Social Care Information Centre makes clear the escalation in the number of anti-depressant drugs:

- In 2014, **51.1 million** items of anti-depressant drugs were dispensed in England.
- This represents a **97.1%** increase on the figures for 2004.
- The increase between 2013 and 2014 was **7.2%**.
- The overall cost of items dispensed has actually fallen by **£135.7 million** since 2014.

The apparent anomaly between the dramatic rise in the number of items dispensed and the overall fall in cost (around 1/3) is certainly, in part, due to a number of the more frequently prescribed drugs coming out of patent and becoming generic. This means that they can be produced more cheaply by other manufacturers who do not have to re-coup the initial cost of the initial research and clinical trials.

Stress in the education profession

So, most of the statistics we have looked at so far have been general to all workers and whilst many of the strategies for managing stress are generic, I am particularly interested in how stress affects the education profession.

Statistics specifically on work-related stress in the education profession are a little harder to come by, but there are one or two useful indicators.

In May 2013, Teachers Assurance Ltd, a financial services provider for teachers, conducted a survey of 735 teachers in conjunction with research specialist Schoolzone. Amongst their findings were:

'**76%** of teachers believed their stress levels were having repercussions on their health.
56% elected that they would definitely be better at their job if they were less stressed.
13.2 days sick leave [on average] are taken per teacher in the UK.'

(Teachers Assurance Company Ltd, 2013)

Try and estimate the missing figures in the following statistics by the Association of Teachers and Lecturers (ATL) in 2014 (answers at the end of the chapter):

ATL surveyed more than 900 education staff about their mental health and the reasons for any problems, ahead of a debate at the union's 2014 conference. The survey found:

- _____**%** of school and college staff have noticed a rise in mental health problems among colleagues in the past two years.
- _____**%** of those working in education feel their job has had a negative impact on their mental health.
- _____**%** of school and college staff hide mental health issues from employers.

The most common factors affecting the mental health of education staff were

- _____**%** pressures to meet targets
- _____**%** inspections
- _____**%** pressure from leaders.

(Association of Teachers and Lecturers, 2014)

A BBC report from 2015 suggests that stress levels among teachers in England's classrooms are soaring.

The report states that unions blame workload for large numbers of staff taking time off work or leaving the profession and that insurance industry data suggests stress is the biggest cause of staff absence except for maternity. *The Guardian* reported on Wednesday 26 December 2012, that:

'The number of teachers taking stress leave has increased by 10% over the past four years, with 15 local authorities seeing a 50% increase in stress-related absences, according to statistics released under the Freedom of Information Act.

(*The Guardian*, 2012)'

The Guardian goes on to report. . .

'Of the 66 local authorities who responded to the Guardian's request for information, 40 saw an increase in the number of teachers taking stress leave between the academic years 2008–9 and 2011–12.'

(*The Guardian*, 2012)

In 2014, an *Education Staff Health Survey* report produced by *The Education Support Partnership* (then called *The Teacher Support Network*) gave the following stark headlines:

1   '**88%** of people working in education have suffered from stress.
2   Just **8%** said they have a wellbeing policy at work that is implemented.
3   **89%** said that workload was the main cause of their mental health issues.
4   **13%** left their job as a result.'

(The Education Support Partnership, 2014)

'These results show how poor mental health at work is destroying the quality of teaching. A significant number of staff are taking time off sick while others who remain at work demonstrate how ill health affects their confidence and performance in the classroom or lecture hall.'

(Julian Stanley, Chief Executive of The Education Support Partnership, 2014)

In 2014, Education Secretary, Nicky Morgan, attempting a slightly more conciliatory approach to the teaching profession than her predecessor (Michael Gove – lest we forget!), announced that The Department for Education (DfE) would run an online *Workload challenge* consultation. This took place between 22 October and 21 November 2014.

It asked three key open questions:

1   Tell us about the unnecessary and unproductive tasks which take up too much of your time. Where do these come from?
2   Send us your solutions and strategies for tackling workload – what works well in your school?
3   What do you think should be done to tackle unnecessary workload – by government, by schools or by others?'

The DfE received 43,832 responses. Three key issues emerged when the analysis of the consultation was published in February 2015. They were, perhaps unsurprisingly: **detail, duplication** and **bureaucracy.**

• **'63%** of respondents stated that the excessive level of detail required made the tasks burdensome.

- **45%** stated that duplication added to the burden of their workload.
- **41%** stated that the over-bureaucratic nature of the work made it burdensome.'
(Workload Challenge: Analysis of teacher consultation responses Research Report, 2015)

The report goes on to state that:

'There were two particular issues that were reported as being burdensome for the majority of sample respondents:
- recording, inputting, monitoring and analysing data **(56%)**
- excessive/depth of marking – detail and frequency and detail required **(53%)'**

'Respondents most commonly said that the burden of their workload was created by:
- accountability/perceived pressures of Ofsted (53%)
- tasks set by senior/middle leaders (51%).'

One suspects that the two go very much hand in hand!

'In line with what respondents thought were the most overly burdensome tasks, the most common solutions they suggested were:
- modify marking arrangements (32%)
- reduce the need for data inputting and analysis (25%)
- increase time for planning, preparation and assessment (25%)
- trust teachers as professionals (24%)
- reduce frequency of curriculum/qualification/examination changes (22%)
- review/change Ofsted processes (21%)'

Take control...

Breathing

People often believe that because breathing is an automatic function we have no control over it, but this is only true up to a point. We do have some control over the way in which we breathe. Breathing correctly can help to optimise our physiological and mental functions.

- Inefficient breathing will lessen the amount of oxygen in our blood stream, which in turn leads to less oxygen reaching the brain.
- Inefficient breathing can raise heart rate and blood pressure leaving us feeling more tense and stressed.
- We naturally breathe from the diaphragm, but when stressed we can fall into two traps:
  1 Hunching our shoulders and contracting our chest cavity – inhaling in short breaths.
  2 Not breathing at all for short periods of time whilst we ruminate or concentrate.

Either will serve to reduce the amount of oxygen in the bloodstream.

- Stress can cause us to breathe inefficiently and inefficient breathing can lead us to become even more stressed and tense. It's a vicious circle that is worth breaking.
- Try the following exercise:
  o Lie flat on your back with one hand spread so that your thumb is below your throat and touching the top of your rib-cage. Your little finger should be reaching down towards your stomach.
  o Stretch your other hand out to cover your stomach, with the thumb of the second hand touching the tip of the little finger of the first hand. The little finger of the second hand should be reaching down in the direction of your toes.
  o If you are breathing efficiently from the diaphragm, you should be able to see the gentle rise and fall of the hand on your stomach but very little movement of the hand on your rib cage.

- When you are feeling stressed or under pressure, check that you are breathing from the diaphragm and not your chest. This is easier to do if you are lying flat or (more probably at work) standing straight rather than sitting in a hunched position.
- Inhale through your nose counting in your head to three. Hold the breath for three seconds before exhaling through the mouth while counting for a further three seconds. Controlling your breathing in this manner will help to steady you leaving you feeling less tense and more in control.
- Practise concentrating on your breathing. Imagine that you have a balloon inside your stomach. When you breathe in the balloon inflates, and when you breathe out it deflates. Notice the sensations as it inflates and deflates. Watch your stomach slowly rising and falling.
- Yawning in public is generally viewed as being socially unacceptable. It is often interpreted as a signal that we are bored with the company of the people we are with or the situation we find ourselves in. However, yawning is actually a very effective way of our bodies signalling the need for increased oxygen and getting it quickly. As increased oxygen intake helps to reduce stress levels, then the next time you feel a yawn coming on (and you are alone), embrace it. Why not try actually engineering one?
- Practise mindful breathing, really concentrating on the sensation of air filling and leaving your lungs.

Leadership interview

Jane Rutherford – Headteacher, King Edward VI School, Lichfield, Staffordshire

Background

King Edward VI is an 11–18 years school serving the small, cathedral city of Lichfield. The school has 1,430 students from both the city itself and surrounding rural areas. Jane is in her seventh year at the school. Having originally been appointed as Deputy Head, she became Acting Head in January 2014 and was appointed to the permanent position the following Easter.

Jane spent three years living and working in Japan, and a year working in France before training to become a teacher and this has helped her to appreciate the importance of both verbal and non-verbal communication, as well as helping to shape her thinking and approach to leadership and management.

Stressors

'Resolving staffing issues can be both unpredictable and quite draining – particularly in periods of change. As a head, you inevitably want to resolve issues correctly and quickly as they not only have an impact on staff but on the students' learning too. The frustration lies in having to make do with situations that are not ideal. This does not sit comfortably.'

Jane also says that dealing with parent issues can also be a source of stress at times.

'Parent issues are very hard to predict. Sometimes there appears to be no reason or rationale and each one is different. They can usually be resolved but it takes time and energy.'

She cites changes in education policy, at a national level as a factor too.

'It is not so much change itself but the pace of change that is frustrating. As a head, you end up having to be the buffer between changes to the curriculum and students to ensure it does not have an impact on them achieving their best.'

Coping strategies

Having spent several years immersed in other cultures, particularly in Japan where there is often no direct translation of words or phrases, Jane recognises the importance of clarity of communication and the potential for misunderstanding. She believes that more often than not, things that go wrong in a school are down to miscommunication at some level.

When things do go wrong, Jane tries to build in the time to review why they have happened, in order to minimise the likelihood of a similar situation occurring again.

'Key tool, is getting the right people in post with the trust and authority to deal with situations.'

Having children of her own helps Jane keep a sense of perspective and makes spending time outside of work an imperative. Jane's partner is a primary headteacher and this gives them both a common perspective as well as an understanding of the late nights and irregular work patterns that headship inevitably involves.

Physical times away, such as family holidays, also help to counteract the pressures of headship.

Managing stress in others

'It's important to be open and honest and, where you can, protect people from the pressures being cascaded down from above.'

Jane stresses the importance of 'joined-up thinking' so that staff can see how things fit together. She is a strong believer in collaboration and in listening to staff and streamlining working practices wherever possible.

'It's important as a leader to stay calm and positive – what you do reflects on others. Things that are unknowns can be scary too. Trying to take the mystery out of situations and processes really does help.'

'People need the freedom to be who they need to be. We are, as a profession, so hard on ourselves. So much of dealing with staff issues is about maintaining lines of communication. As head, you will not always be the person that they will feel most comfortable talking to

but it is so important to open and keep lines of communication open. You need to encourage people to make changes that are within their own control but also be prepared to make short-term adjustments as a leader.'

Advice to new headteachers or other senior leaders

'Don't try and do everything yourself – work as a team to establish your priorities and work towards them together. Try to see the bigger picture and break the School Improvement Plan into small steps so that you can see progress towards your long-term goals.'

Jane also stresses the importance of talking with colleagues and having the confidence to sometimes say 'no' without feeling guilty.

'Statistically, it is clear that many professionals are at risk of leaving in the first few years. Working with less experienced staff, particularly those contemplating the first steps into leadership, is essential to gaining an understanding of the role of leader and the expectations, both of oneself and of the school.'

Summary: Chapter 2

- Stress is consistently one of the most commonly reported types of work-related illness.
- In Great Britain, stress accounts for nearly half of all work-related illnesses.
- Whilst there is no compelling evidence that the overall number of cases of work-related stress is going up, there is evidence that cases amongst those working in education are on the increase.
- Education professionals are the second-highest occupation at risk of work-related stress.
- Many people are fearful of reporting mental health issues.
- Three quarters of teachers believe their stress levels are having repercussions on their health.
- The demands of the education system for excessive detail, bureaucracy and duplication of tasks are at the heart of teachers' workload difficulties.

ATL Survey Answers

- **'38%** of school and college staff have noticed a rise in mental health problems among colleagues in the past two years.
- **55%** of those working in education feel their job has had a negative impact on their mental health.
- **68%** school and college staff hide mental health issues from employers.'

'The most common factors affecting the mental health of education staff were

- **63%** pressures to meet targets
- **59%** inspections
- **55%** pressure from leaders.'

Score yourself 10 points if you were within a five percent variance of the answer and 5 points if within a ten percent variance of the answer.

How well did you do?

Try asking the same questions of colleagues – it's a good way of opening up a debate about a difficult subject.

3 The tipping point – Can stress be good?

Challenges are what make life interesting and overcoming them is what makes life meaningful.

Joshua J. Marine

Work-related stress can be defined as:

> *'The adverse reaction people have to excessive pressure or other types of demand placed on them at work.'* Health and Safety Executive

Pressure is part of work. It helps to keep us motivated and can improve our performance. However, excessive or unrelenting pressure can lead to stress and have a negative effect on performance. Stress is therefore a response to pressure. It can be costly to employers, but more importantly, it can make people ill. A good understanding of the nature of stress is central to maintaining our own personal resilience and to leading others effectively.

Throughout each and every day, we experience pressures to fulfil either our own needs or the needs of others, e.g. the need to get up so that we are not late for work, the need to meet performance management targets in order to progress up the pay scale or even to fit in a trip to the supermarket after work in order to buy tea to feed the vultures back home! The pressures and demands of modern life can often cause us stress.

So what is stress?

We all have a perfectly natural physiological response to perceived threats that has been programmed into us from the days when our ancestors lived in caves and hunted for food. When we feel under threat, our nervous system responds by releasing a wave of stress hormones, including adrenaline and cortisol, in order to rouse our bodies ready to respond. Our hearts beat faster, blood pressure rises and oxygen is pumped to the muscles in our extremities, reaction times quicken and we become more focussed. The caveman (or woman) version of us is now prepared for one of two options – fight or flight.

Fight – '*I can take on my attacker and win!*'
or
Flight – '*I need to run from my attacker in order to survive!*'

The body's inbuilt stress response is designed to protect us and keep us safe, ensuring that we die another day.

As I was writing this chapter, the UK was experiencing the tail end of Hurricane Bertha, which brought a month's worth of rainfall in 24 hours. Eddie, my golden retriever, is no respecter of rainfall – loving water is a characteristic of the breed. So I piled him into the back of my Ford Mondeo estate this morning with a view to a soggy hike across some nearby fields. As I pulled on to the roundabout by our local supermarket in the driving rain, three things happened:

1   In the poor conditions I failed to notice the car entering the roundabout to my right (which I should have given way to and was now descending upon me at some speed);
2   I stalled my Mondeo on the roundabout, in the direct path of the oncoming car.
3   I felt a sense of panic and a surge of adrenaline. I turned the key, fearing the worst, but then I experienced a wave of relief as the diesel engine surged to life and propelled me away from certain death. (I studied drama at university, so I am allowed to be dramatic!)

It is amazing in situations like this, and I am sure you will have experienced something similar, just how much action can be condensed into what is, in reality, only a split second. This is our stress response working to good effect.

Travel back in time thirty years and you find me at university appearing as Lysander, one of the four lovers, in Shakespeare's *A Midsummer Night's Dream*.

- **Good point**: It was in traditional dress – I can't bear needless updating. (I once saw a production of *Romeo and Juliet* where the Montagues and the Capulets were fighting for control of a petrol tanker that was on stage. Oh please! Really?)
- **Not so good point:** It was Shakespeare, so my usual learning only an approximation of a script was not going to cut the mustard here.
- **Not so good point:** It was theatre in the round – the audience are all around you in a circle, so no scope for my usual technique of writing the bogey lines I could never remember on pieces of masking tape and hiding them around the set. (Ask anyone I have ever acted with and they will confirm this to be true – it was like the final part of seventies TV programme, *The Generation Game*.)

As it turned out, the lack of any actual set proved even more unforgiving when the actor playing Demetrius stepped on the hem of Hermia's skirt. Blissfully unaware, she stepped away leaving her skirt behind and revealing underwear that was a little anachronistic to say the least. With nowhere to hide, Hermia was forced to try and reassemble her costume (and her dignity) whilst, in a surge of adrenaline, Demetrius and I feigned dialogue to cover the lengthy pause that the Bard had certainly not written but was sufficiently convincing to fool most of the audience, some of whom thought it was part of the play. (Not so our senior tutor, but that's another story!)

Recently, a man slipped and fell and became trapped in the gap between a railway platform and a train in Western Australia. I witnessed it on the news half a world away. In that potentially lethal, adrenaline-charged and highly stressful situation other passengers' natural instinct to help kicked in. They collectively 'rocked' the train away from the platform releasing the man.

My point? Stressful situations can produce some very positive outcomes.

Whilst I have always loved performing (perhaps with the exception of the time I was asked to mime being a woolly jumper in a washing machine in an audition), I have always suffered badly from stage fright. However stressful the situation may be, I actually need that surge of adrenaline to perform well. Even now, when delivering keynote speeches and workshops, I still get very nervous beforehand. The one time since I started working as a presenter that I did not experience that physiological reaction to stress, it turned out to be the session from hell, where nothing seemed to go right, my laptop would not interface with the projector and my timings were out. I was cross with myself more than anything else and could not wait to get out of there.

I recently asked happiness expert, Andy Cope, if he still got nervous after nearly ten years on the road talking about positive psychology. Andy is so natural and looks so relaxed when delivering. So does he still get nervous? 'Every time', he replied.

Stress can be a good thing in small doses – it can help you perform well under pressure and motivate you to give your best. The stress response can actually help you rise to meet challenges.

Mostly our stress response is proportionate to the perceived level of threat. Most of us find job interviews a stressful situation and our 'fight or flight' stress response kicks in. When I was interviewed for my second headship, the process took place over two days, as is often the case. I spent the whole two days with a faint veil of perspiration on my forehead, I could not eat and felt nauseous. I spent the time between interviews giving presentations, handling performance data, meeting the School Council, pacing the school corridors and wearing the carpets out. This was not a life-threatening situation. I never seriously thought of physically pummelling the interview panel or fleeing the building. However, there was a *level of threat*.

In these situations, no one wants to make a fool of themselves or lose the job on the basis of an unfortunate comment made under pressure, a poorly answered question, or failure to spot a glaringly obvious flaw in performance data. The perceived threat is to our confidence, our reputation and to how others might view us. It is why it makes applying for an internal position within a school so much more difficult. If you are not successful, you still have to face people the following day.

In the late 1980s, our LEA had a residential conference centre with very limited facilities and dormitory style accommodation. As a young teacher, I applied (unsuccessfully) for my first senior leadership position. The interviews had been on the Thursday and I was looking forward to a weekend course on science and technology at the residential centre where I could lick the wounds to my ego. Imagine my delight at finding the head who had just failed to appoint me, sleeping two feet away from me for two nights. In fairness, I can't imagine he was too chuffed either. It was toe-curlingly embarrassing.

When working properly, our stress response is graduated to the level of threat that we perceive. It is our body and our mind's way of protecting us from harm. However, our ancestors were only ever protecting themselves from short-term threats such as physical attack (hence the 'fight or flight' adrenaline-surged response). Whilst the nature and frequency of threats to our well-being have changed over the centuries, our stress responses have failed to keep pace with the times and remain the same.

In my first year of teaching, I taught an ill-conceived topic on the Industrial Revolution. In the difficult, and often appalling, working conditions that characterised many factories at that time, losing a limb in unguarded machinery was a common occurrence. Fortunately, most working environments are now far safer from a physical point of view. I did have a member of staff trip whilst carrying a pile of books once – she did jar her back quite badly. But, with the exception of a handful of tragic circumstances, that is the extent of the physical threat posed to our well-being.

However, working in a school can pose a wide range of non-physical threats to our well-being.

- Pupils challenging our authority
- Unreasonable demands from parents
- Promotion into a role for which we have had little training
- Unrealistic targets imposed from above
- Moving deadlines
- Excessive workload
- Anticipation of inspection outcomes
- Changes to performance management arrangements

These are just a handful of the potential, non-physical, threats to our well-being.

The difficulty is that our physical stress response system was designed for a *short-term* response to a *physical* threat. In the current climate, in schools and elsewhere, the threats to our well-being are neither physical, nor short term, eliciting a medium to high-level stress response on an ongoing basis. Living a life where our bodies and minds are in a near permanent state of stress response inevitably takes its toll on us and, for some, the effects can be far reaching, both at work and at home.

We are all individuals with different tolerance levels to the mental demands that are placed on us. Some people seem to positively thrive under pressure, whilst others experience anxiety and/or risk sliding into depression. Some of us hit problems when our stress response becomes disproportionate to the level of threat. Let me give you an example of what I mean...

In October 1979, I was flying back with my parents from Majorca to East Midlands Airport at the end of what would be my final foreign holiday with them.

The 17-year-old me was feeling a little sore, as it was the holiday on which I had discovered *happy hour* away from my parents and on my return to the hotel had misjudged the location of the hotel steps and fallen into a cactus bed. 'Did you feel stupid?' you ask. To which I inevitably reply, 'Yes, I felt a bit of a p***k.' (Sorry – had to be done.)

The aeroplane was in British airspace when the pilot announced over the tannoy that, due to a problem with one of the engines, we were having to divert to Luton. It was of course, 'nothing to be concerned about'. I was momentarily reassured until the plane banked very steeply in what appeared to be a U-turn in a manoeuvre that would suggest that the pilot had previously flown for the Red Arrows. I can remember gripping the armrests tightly (as if that would make any difference), and offering a silent prayer to the Almighty. I was convinced our number was up (clearly it wasn't or you would not be reading this). There had been engine failure. My legs were like jelly as we walked across the car park at Luton to board the bus that would eventually take us back to East Midlands and I contemplated my perceived brush with death.

It was some fifteen years before I flew again. After I got married and we had three small children, we tended to holiday with friends and family in the beautiful and unspoilt village of Aberporth, in Cardigan Bay in Wales. Thus, I had no occasion to fly. It was easier in many ways with three young children. But, looking back it was partly an avoidance strategy on my part.

When the time came to fly again I was terrified even though I knew that, statistically, flying was one of the safest ways to travel. I would quite happily have returned home, but with quite a lot of coercion (and two double Scotches) I eventually made it on board the aeroplane. My stress reaction was based on one unfortunate event back in 1979 when we had not even crashed! My physical reactions were disproportionate to the realistic level of threat posed by flying.

I have flown a number of times since and tolerance of the stress has improved each time with increased exposure to the threat to my well-being. I am not a great flier; my family would still rather not sit next to me because of the embarrassment of being associated with the man who clings to the armrests at the first sign of turbulence.

As my friend Nick, a very seasoned international flier, once said to me after a bumpy landing: 'James, any landing where you are able to walk away from the plane is a good landing!'

Avoidance is a very common reaction to stress, but not a very helpful one in the long run.

This is why drivers who have been involved in a motoring accident are usually advised to get behind the wheel of a car again as soon as possible. The longer you leave it, the bigger the mountain to climb.

Central to us being able to thrive is our perception of our own abilities and whether we can successfully respond to the perceived demands being placed upon us.

When faced with a perceived threat, or demand, our mind analyses the situation. Professor Terry Looker and Olga Gregson, a senior lecturer in the Department of Biological Sciences at Manchester Metropolitan University suggest that we can interpret a situation in one of three ways:

- **"I can cope with this situation"** – perceived coping ability outweighs perceived demands
- **"I am not sure if I can cope with this situation"** – doubt about perceived ability to cope with perceived demands
- **"I cannot cope with this situation"** – perceived demands outweigh perceived coping ability

(Looker and Gregson, 1997)

Think of coping as a see-saw with the demands made upon us at one end, and our perceived ability to respond to those demands at the other. Provided the demands on us do not exceed our perceived ability to cope, the see-saw remains balanced and we maintain an inner equilibrium. However, once we perceive the demands on us to be greater than our ability to deliver, we experience a stress reaction. Staying in that state for a prolonged period of time can leave us feeling overwhelmed as well as having a very negative effect on our mental and physical health.

The 'tipping point' between coping and not coping with stress is different for each and every one of us, but we will all have one. No one is invincible.

Our ability to keep the see-saw in balance is based on a whole series of factors including our genetic make-up, past experiences, support networks and belief systems.

Connie Lillas, a psychologist, uses a driving analysis to describe three ways that people commonly respond when they are overwhelmed by stress. This particularly resonates with me because, at different times in my career, I have reacted in all three ways.

Foot on the accelerator – an agitated or fight stress response. Overly emotional and agitated.

Foot on the brake – a withdrawn, depressed or flight stress response. Shut down withdrawn, and show little emotion.

Feet on both pedals – you become frozen and can't do anything. Under the surface you are extremely agitated.

Over the years I have come to realise that it is not the situations themselves that are stressful, it is our reaction to them that makes us feel anxious or distressed. What might be deemed a stressful situation by one person could be a situation in which another person thrives.

> Three or four years ago whilst on a flight to Dublin with my friend Nick (the seasoned international flyer mentioned previously who has travelled all over the world with his job), we encountered some turbulence. I experienced that gut-wrenching sensation of your stomach dropping away as the plane was buffeted and felt a surge of panic. I gripped those armrests and mentally replayed the cabin crew's pre-flight safety briefing. As beads of sweat appeared on my brow, I opened my eyes and looked two rows nearer the front on the aisle seat. There was Nick (he won't sit with me either!), reading the newspaper looking completely unperturbed. He didn't even look up.
>
> Same situation – two completely different responses.

Recognising that it is our responses that cause us stress is an important step in taking back some control.

To return to the see-saw analogy for a moment. If the see-saw is out of balance and the perceived demands on you (also known as stressors) outweigh your perceived ability to meet them, then there are realistically two options open to you:

1 Eliminate or at least reduce the demand or stressor.
2 Retrain your brain to respond in a more positive way to the demand or stressor.

It is sometimes possible to find ways to eliminate or reduce a source of stress in our private lives. For example, I know a lady called Martha who found herself feeling increasingly claustrophobic in the busy aisles of her local supermarket. This brought on a sense of panic whenever she thought about going. She was able to eliminate this stressor by doing most of her shopping online and having the food delivered to her house.

I once read about a man who had panic attacks in the cinema but could not put his finger on why it happened. He removed the stressor by not going to the cinema and waiting for films to come out on DVD instead. It was a nuisance waiting three months for the DVD release, but it was not going to ruin his life.

Similarly, with acquaintances or even family members that wind you up, you can take some control over when you see them.

However, elimination or reduction of stressors in school, or any other work place, can be far more problematic. Consider these three examples:

1 Lesson observations – being observed teaching *can* feel quite threatening (depending on the manner in which the observation is carried out) but observation is a requirement we cannot opt out of.
2 Targets – we may feel the pressure of the targets set for pupil progress but cannot avoid them.
3 Colleagues – a particular colleague may really annoy us by the things that they say, but we have to see them each and every day.

We might be able to modify some of our work-based stressors to a degree, but there are others, such as an Ofsted inspection, that we simply cannot avoid.

In order to keep the see-saw balanced, our best option is to retrain our brains to respond more positively to the stressors and increase our resilience.

In his book, *Find Your Power*, Chris Johnstone makes a useful analogy that resilience is like the sea level that keeps our rowing boat afloat. When our resilience is depleted, the sea level goes down exposing far more rocks and other dangers on which our boat may flounder.

Whilst this book concentrates on work-related stress, it would be simplistic to suggest other life events have no effect on our resilience at work. The death of a family member, break up of a relationship or financial debt, to name but a few, can all serve to reduce our sea level and make us more susceptible to the pressures at work.

It is also true that some people are more susceptible to stress than others. Type 'A' personalities tend to be less patient and more competitive, whereas type 'B' personalities tend to be more relaxed and laid-back in their approach. Most people exhibit some traits of both but to see which is the best fit for you, try taking this test.

Challenge: Personality test

Do you have a type 'A' or a type 'B' personality?

Tick the boxes that most closely apply to you.

Type 'A'	Type 'B'
☐ Hold feelings in	☐ Freely express feelings
☐ Competitive	☐ Not competitive
☐ Impatient when waiting	☐ Can wait calmly
☐ Perfectionist	☐ Can live with something not being quite perfect
☐ Tend to work on several things at once without completing	☐ Tend to work on one thing at once
☐ Tend to rush tasks	☐ Tend to take time over tasks
☐ Usually take work home	☐ Rarely take work home
☐ Tend to talk quickly	☐ Slow, measured speech
☐ Tend to interrupt conversations and finish other people's sentences	☐ Can listen and let other people finish their sentences
☐ Arrive at appointments late or just in time	☐ Arrive at appointments with time to spare
☐ Limited social life and interests	☐ Good social life and variety of interests
☐ Generally dissatisfied with work	☐ Generally satisfied with work
☐ Generally dissatisfied with life	☐ Generally satisfied with life

So are you more of a type 'A' or a type 'B' person?

You probably won't be too surprised to learn that type 'A's are a little more prone to suffer from stress than type 'B's.

The very nature of teaching in schools can push more into type 'A' behaviour. I don't know many teachers who are afforded the luxury of working on one thing at once. Most teachers regularly bring work home with them, and this can limit social lives and outside interests. It is little wonder that education is such a high-risk occupation when it comes to work-related stress.

However, the good news is that type 'A's are able to retrain their thinking to be less competitive and to be able to relax, which in return reduces stress.

'So even if you feel that you are "the worrying type" or have "always been a worrier", you can anticipate being able to change your outlook and the way you feel in yourself.' (Helen Kennerley, 1997, 2009)

So what are the main stressors as perceived by professionals working in schools today?

In Summer 2014, as part of the conference speeches and workshop sessions I was running on leadership and stress management, I surveyed an audience of 100 people made up of a mixture of headteachers, deputy heads and other senior leaders. Each group was asked to list their top five stressors. Whilst there is some correlation between the results, there are differences too. The results are listed from 1–5 with 1 being the highest cause of stress.

Top 5 stressors for headteachers

1 External accountabilities such as Ofsted and HMI inspections
2 Resolving staffing issues
3 Pupil achievement targets
4 Overall workload
5 Issues with parents

Top 5 stressors for deputy headteachers

1 Pupil achievement targets
2 External accountabilities such as Ofsted and HMI inspections
3 Issues with parents
4 Resolving staffing issues
5 Pupil behaviour

Top 5 stressors for other senior leaders

1 Overall workload
2 Pupil achievement targets
3 Issues with parents
4 External accountabilities such as Ofsted and HMI inspections
5 Pupil behaviour

Do the responses surprise you?

It is clear, that whilst many of the same issues cause school leaders stress, the pressures are different depending on role and responsibilities. As a head, one of my most significant stressors was also the anticipation of an inspection; what it would mean for the school as a whole and for me personally. However, it would be a mistake even amongst school leaders, to assume that our biggest stressors are the same.

When feeling over-whelmed by the pressures of work, it is often helpful to break down and grade the stress we experience in order to gain a better understanding of what we are feeling.

Challenge

Look at each of the areas below and attach a score for the degree to which it causes you stress.

0 = no stress   1= slightly stressful   2 = moderately stressful
3 = very stressful   4 = highly stressful

Stressor	Score
Relationship with another colleague(s)	
Relationship with line manager/governors (e.g. lack of support)	
Relationships with parents	
Behaviour of a pupil(s)	
Recognition of efforts and achievements	
Staffing levels	
Ofsted inspection	
Imposed targets	
Changes to policy and curriculum	
Professional development opportunities	
Opportunities for progression	
Work–life balance	
Rate of pay	
Physical working environment	

Score out of 56

Most people will be scoring around 15–20 as we all suffer from degrees of stress which may not be affecting ability to continue working. Chris would suggest a score of 20–26 would prompt a discussion with line manager/ mentor and scores over 26 should lead to advice to see your GP.

What are your most significant stressors and how do they compare with those of other school leaders with similar levels of responsibility?

Take control . . .

Sleep

People vary greatly in terms of the amount of sleep that they need in order to function well. Most people have difficulties in sleeping at times, and some studies suggest that around a third of the adult population are affected by sleep problems. People experiencing sleep problems tend to fall into two categories:

1   Those who have difficulty getting off to sleep.
2   Those who get off to sleep but then wake in the night and ruminate for hours.

It is true that, as we get older, we tend to sleep less deeply and require less sleep. We can never guarantee a good night's sleep but we can try and stack the cards in our favour.

- Avoid checking emails and using your tablet or laptop for at least an hour before going to bed.
- Avoid caffeine after 7pm.
- Drinking alcohol close to bedtime can help you to fall asleep quickly, but can lead to periods of wakefulness in the night.
- Whilst exercise is good, avoid exercising too close to bedtime.
- Milk contains natural sedatives, so hot milky drinks not only return us to childhood, they calm us too.
- Try having a bowl of cereal before bedtime.
- Try herbal teabags with valerian, which is a natural sedative.
- A hot bath, or even a shower, helps to relax tight muscles brought on by the stresses of the day.
- Essential oils added to your bath or spotted on to a pillow, handkerchief or cloth, can make a surprising difference to your ability to sleep. Try lavender, camomile or marjoram.
- Keep a notepad and pen by your bedside so that if you do wake you can commit thoughts to paper without having to hold them in your mind.
- Make sure your room is well ventilated and neither too hot nor too cold.

- Sounds of ocean waves are very calming and mimic breathing patterns when calm.
- Play these, if only through earphones at bedtime or if you wake at night. Try the CDs, *Ocean Waves at Sunset* or *Relax with Nature volume 3: Natural Sounds*, or any of the number of great free apps available, e.g. try *Relax melodies* by Ipnos Soft.
- Rather than counting sheep, try counting backwards slowly from 500 in time with your breathing. Counter-intuitively, it works.
- When you are struggling to sleep, try progressive relaxation. Start imagining your toes relaxed and work up your body.
- Lots of people wake in the night. If you have an alarm clock, particularly a digital one that glows the time, keep it covered to avoid the 'it's not worth going back to sleep now' syndrome.
- If you do wake, don't ruminate. Keep your mind occupied by plugging in your earphones and listening to a radio, CD player or ipod. BBC Radio iPlayer is a great distraction – particularly comedy.
- Keep to a regular bedtime and waking up time routine.
- When you can't sleep or when you wake up in the night, don't make going back to sleep your goal. It puts pressure on you. Instead, make your goal to relax and you will often find that sleep follows.

Leadership interview

Sue Goodall – Headteacher, Long Lane Church of England Primary School, Ashbourne, Derbyshire

Background

Sue has spent seventeen years as headteacher of the same village primary school. Long Lane has 46 pupils spread across two classes: a Foundation Stage/Year 1/ Year 2 class and another comprising Years 3–6. Sue herself has a three-day teaching commitment each week.

Stressors

Looking back over her time as head of a small school, Sue says the biggest and most consistent stressor has been overall workload and juggling the demands of her teaching commitment along with the management side of the role of a teaching head. It can be a feat of juggling and having to accept that there are times when the teaching has to be top priority and management issues have to go more on the back burner. Similarly, when preparing for meetings with the LEA School Improvement Officer, where progress data and target setting are being discussed, you simply do have to make this a priority, as the importance of the meeting has implications for everyone working in the school.

An increase in secretarial support in recent years has helped with the issue of workload but there are still times when deadlines loom and when OK has to be good enough. You cannot constantly beat yourself up.

Although overall workload has been the biggest and most consistent stressor, working in a small school can magnify other issues. Sue says that she has been very fortunate over the years to have a very supportive school community, but in the rare cases where relationships with a set of parents have become strained this has caused a lot of stress. The nature of a small school community is that figuratively 'there is nowhere to hide'.

Coping strategies

Despite the many time constraints of the job, Sue has maintained attending exercise classes regularly and finds that helps to reduce tension. Having a partner who is a retired teacher with many years of experience also helps.

> 'I am able to offload and use him as a sounding board. He understands the issues without being directly involved. Relaxing with a glass of wine helps too.'

Managing stress in others

Like many other heads, when Sue has a member of staff who she knows is feeling the pressure, she tends to take on more herself and pass less on. However, she cites one of the advantages of working in a small school environment as being:

> 'Staff can sit down and say, "OK, this is going wrong, what collectively, can we do to support one another and fix this situation?" Equally, staff will sometimes come to me and say, "You look a bit snowed under at the moment, what can we do to help?" There is never a culture of blame. Good relationships are of key importance.'

Sue feels it is very important that situations are not allowed to drag on indefinitely and giving support with a timescale is important, e.g. 'What can I take off you for the next four weeks?' or 'Would it help to go home straight away at the end of the school day for the next week?'

Sometimes, though, Sue says that enough simply has to be enough.

Advice to new headteachers or other senior leaders

> 'We always draw a line under each day with the pupils and treat the new day as a fresh start. We should be kind and cut ourselves the same slack.'

> 'So much depends on the environment you work in and that in turn depends on great relationships with the children, staff, parents and governors – work hard to get these right.'

> 'Try not to take things personally but look to see the bigger picture.'

Summary: Chapter 3

- Pressure is a feature of all work. Work-related stress is an adverse reaction to excessive pressure.
- Stress is a physiological response designed for short-term 'fight or flight'.
- Stress *can* keep us safe and help us perform well.
- When working properly, stress responses should be graduated to the level of perceived threat.
- The pressures that cause us stress are generally referred to as 'stressors'.

- Our stress response systems are not geared up for non-physical or long-term pressures.
- Many stressors in education are neither physical nor short-term.
- Long-term stress reactions can have an adverse effect on physical and mental health.
- Type 'A' personalities can be more susceptible to stress but can retrain their thinking.
- Whilst many education professionals have the same stressors, the level of impact can vary according to role and responsibilities.
- Understanding and recognising stress tolerance in ourselves and others is of great importance in maintaining our own resilience as well as that of our colleagues.

---

4 The only way is up! – Getting back on your feet

The darkest hour is truly just before the dawn.

Proverb

Back to my story...

After a week of absence from work, I needed to go to the doctor to obtain a sick note. The searing spasms of pain that I had been experiencing had subsided, although I was still experiencing regular twinges. I felt most comfortable in bed and so that was where I was now spending most of my time, cocooned in my duvet. Looking back, perhaps I was confusing feeling comfortable with feeling safe. I felt safe in bed. I had a bad back, I was not very well and nobody realistically could expect me to do anything, not even walk the dog and certainly not make the myriad of decisions that were expected of me every day at work.

So there I was, in early February 2007 sitting in my GP's consulting room. My wife, Rachel, had taken me there, partly because I did not want to walk through the village and risk being seen by people who I knew (particularly parents from school), but also to support me and make sure I actually went. It was supposed to be a five–ten minute consultation although it seemed much, much longer. For much of the time, I stared at the floor too embarrassed at the state I was in and unable to maintain eye contact with my doctor. I tried to talk about feeling overwhelmed by the pressures of work but, characteristically the stammer kicked in and I became frustrated and tearful. He was kind, supportive and helpful and gave me more than my allotted time, which would certainly have knocked back his appointments for the rest of the morning.

The doctor reassured me that I was far from alone in what I was experiencing and that he was seeing an increasing number of class teachers and senior leaders in education who were also struggling to cope with the demands of the job. He asked my wife to come into the room so that she could hear what he had to say as he could tell that I was struggling to stay focussed. He gently chastised me for not having come to see him sooner and for letting things build up to this point. He said that we needed a two-pronged approach: firstly, to attempt to address some of the physical symptoms and then to look at some of the underlying causes. The fact that he used the word 'we' was so reassuring. He was in it *with* me and was going to help me – that was the message I took from what he was saying.

He prescribed me some stronger painkillers that I could take when my back was going into spasm (although it had continued to do that, it was never with the same intensity of pain that I had experienced on my first day of absence from work). He also advocated that I should put a cold compress on the muscles on my back to reduce the swelling. Secondly, he prescribed a course of mirtazapine, which should both help to stabilise my mood but also to help me sleep. I had not experienced any quality sleep in months. I would either lie awake for two or three hours before drifting off or I would go to sleep and then wake worrying about something I needed to do or remember. The doctor warned me that it would take a good two weeks for the medication to be properly absorbed into my system and for me to start to feel any benefits.

The doctor also felt that I would benefit from a course of therapy with Chris Roome, the mental health therapist who was then based at the surgery, to help look at the underlying causes of what I was experiencing. However, he also said that I was currently too unwell to benefit. He explained that in terms of my mental well-being, I was currently right at the bottom of a very large U-shaped curve.

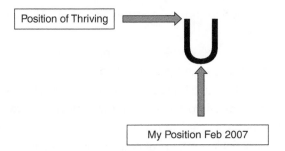

In order for the therapy to have the best chance of success, my mental state needed to improve so that I had started to move away from that bottom point – my lowest ebb.

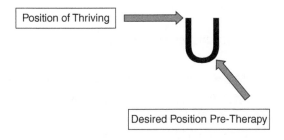

For the next two to three weeks I laid low. I did not really venture out of the house. I think in all honesty that I have always worried too much about what other people think of me. If I cared less, life would certainly have been easier back then. I was desperately concerned about being seen out and about and how people would judge me, given that I was not at work.

When stressed, anxious or depressed, many people's comfort zone seems to shrink. My comfort zone had shrunk to such a degree that I now only felt safe inside the house.

I whiled away my time watching the DVD box set of the extended edition of *The Lord of the Rings* trilogy. There are hours and hours of extras in that set which I will probably never watch again, but for which I was hugely grateful at the time! I also revisited all six existing *Star Wars* films, nine *Star Trek* films and the *Back to the Future* trilogy. Unknowingly at the time, I was engaging in a strategy to avoid thinking about work. By following an extended story narrative I was occupying my mind, preventing my thoughts drifting towards the unwelcome prospect of a return to the very stressors that had led me to this position. (The recurring theme of my film choice was one of escapism, of life in another world or in another time.)

I revisited my GP a couple of weeks later and I was able to report that I had started to sleep a little better and that my mood had improved slightly, but I had become very agitated about 24 hours prior to seeing him. I now know, with the clarity brought by distance from the event, my distress was brought about by the thought that he might declare me fit to work. It was an irrational fear, as I was clearly having difficulty getting out of the house let alone getting into work. However, in my state of mind back then, I was extremely irrational. I remember the doctor writing me a sick note for another month and feeling a huge sense of relief as if some great weight had been lifted from my shoulders. The verification that he too felt that I was too unwell to work somehow took the decision away from me and this is a crucial point:

I had surrendered control and responsibility over my life.

I saw all the things that were troubling me and causing me stress as things that were happening *to* me or things that were being done *to* me.

This is what American psychologist, Martin Seligman describes as 'learned helplessness' in his book Learned Helplessness: *A Theory for the Age of Personal Control* (1995).

The magnitude of the demands at work was overwhelming and I perceived that I was powerless to change that. My mind relinquished all control and my body finally reacted to the massive unreleased symptoms of stress.

My doctor felt that I had reached a point where cognitive behavioural therapy would now be a good step forward and arranged for me to meet with Chris Roome. When we met, a week or two later, I felt an immediate rapport with him and felt that he was someone that I could trust. We met fortnightly for several months but he made me realise several important things early on:

- that my recovery was going to take time;
- that I had got to want to recover;
- that we needed to change some of my behaviours, ways of thinking and habits;
- that I needed to concentrate on taking small steps and not concentrate on the enormity of going back to work.

I am writing this chapter overlooking the sea in Aberporth in Cardigan Bay in Wales. It is beautiful, but the sea looks cold. I have never been one for swimming much in the sea, even when our children were young. If you told me now that I *had to* swim from here across the Irish Sea I would not even attempt it. The magnitude of the task would be too great and my mind would go into defence mode, looking to protect me from the stress and physical threats of a perceived impossible demand.

Ask me to paddle in the sea with you though and that would seem a more realistic prospect. Sure, the water still looks cold but my mind would be saying that it thinks both it and my body could cope with the demands likely to be made of them.

Having persuaded me to paddle, I have now found the water is not as cold as I feared. You could probably persuade me to put on my trunks and wade in up to my waist. (If you were entertaining any Daniel Craig image of a man in Speedos, please park the thought – you would be hugely disappointed!) Having got as far as my waist, I would probably realise that I might as well go the whole hog and would begin swimming. With a building confidence, who knows one day I might even attempt the English Channel! (Still not sure about the Irish Sea though – a little too far perhaps).

'Don't underestimate small steps. It is only a small step which will get you closer to where you want to be tomorrow.'

Unknown

For some time after I went off sick, I was actually unsure whether I wanted 'to get back in the ring and go an extra ten rounds' or not. As my mood stabilised a little more and I finally got some quality sleep, I began to see things a little more rationally and came to the conclusion that I did want to return. I cannot deny that one of the key drivers was financial; I had three kids to put through university over the next few years. But actually, fundamentally, I still loved my job and the school community and I still saw it as my mission to make a positive difference to children's lives. Once I knew that and had reaffirmed it in my own mind then the path ahead became clearer.

Now, with Chris's help, I needed to clarify what small steps I needed to take to get where I wanted to be.

Chris was able to spend time in our sessions gathering information through gentle questioning and came to the conclusion that, whilst I was certainly depressed, my symptoms and behaviours pointed to heightened levels of anxiety as being the main root of my difficulties.

Of particular concern to him was my refusal to leave the house unless compelled to attend medical appointments. I knew that this was a fundamental problem I needed to address, not least of which was because other members of the family had taken over dog walking duties. They had all been very good about this, particularly given that my irrational behaviour had caused me to be extremely intolerant of them at times. (For the record, and in print, I truly apologise for this!)

Chris told me recently, when we met up for a coffee to talk about how the book was going, that he thought that Hector, our golden retriever at the time, had been the saving of me in some respects. Recognising the unfairness of expecting other people to walk him when I was sitting at home doing very little, I decided to do something about it and began to take him out for walks. To begin with, I would get him into the boot of our estate car and drive him to parkland close (but not too close) to where we lived. I would then put on a black woolly hat, which I would pull down to eye level to disguise my features and would start to walk. There is no doubt that the change of scenery, fresh air and exercise certainly helped to lift my spirits after several weeks of self-imposed isolation. Feeling somewhat emboldened by my success with dog walking, I was next encouraged to tackle the weekly shop. Logically, I would have gone to the closest supermarket – less than two minutes away and easily walkable. However, this was also the closest large supermarket to the village where I worked and so was frequented by many families from school. Whilst a very large majority of our parents were pleasant, friendly and supportive people, I was not yet ready to face them, particularly out shopping. My answer was to drive 15 miles to another branch of the same supermarket where I was unlikely to bump into anyone I knew. It was a half-day expedition! It was a hypermarket with so much choice – the pet food aisle alone seemed to go on for miles and miles and I do remember having a meltdown early on because I just could not find the particular brand of cat food that our highly particular cats preferred. I stood in the aisle feeling helpless, unsure of what to do and tears welled in my eyes.

However, as the weeks went by I started to organise my thoughts and plan my route around the store, otherwise it would have taken all day! This may not seem a significant thing, but my concentration was so poor and I think it was more than coincidence that two out of three of the minor road accidents I have had in over thirty years of driving took place around this time.

I also remember my former deputy head and friend, Richard Gerver, taking me to the cinema to see Simon Pegg and Nick Frost in the comedy *Hot Fuzz* at the local cinema. Once inside, and feeling able to remove my disguise of reading glasses and yes, you guessed it, black woolly hat, I found myself enjoying the film. In fact I actually found myself laughing for the first time in months. It was as if someone had opened a shutter and let light come streaming in, only for my subconscious mind to slam it shut again afterwards! I felt guilty – guilty for having laughed and enjoyed myself.

I took up painting watercolours again for the first time since I started teaching. I was very out of practice and I would become very frustrated if I made an irretrievable mistake, but spending some time painting each morning brought some structure to my day and started to help me concentrate again for extended periods.

What Chris was partly doing, although I did not fully appreciate it at the time, was treating a social phobia.

Much of the treatment of stress, anxiety and depression revolves around the issue of avoidance.

In my case, I was *avoiding* situations where I had to interact with other people. I had actually confined my interactions to immediate family only, and even then I was intolerant. So why was I avoiding such interactions? It wasn't that I was avoiding all people – I could interact with the checkout assistants at the hypermarket 15 miles away without the slightest stammer, yet I could not face the possibility of facing anyone I knew in its sister store only two minutes away.

The answers only became clear to me a few months ago when Chris and I were dispassionately reviewing my behaviour to help me gain a better understanding for the writing of this book. Chris gave me two words:

'Shame' *and* 'Guilt'

I certainly would not have been ready to hear those words in 2007 but as soon as he said them to me in 2014 it was as if a light bulb had come on. *That was exactly it.* I was the headteacher of the largest primary school in the county and one of the largest in the UK. It was a position that others had also fought hard at interview to achieve, but yet people had put their faith in me to carry out the role and lead the school on to new and even greater heights. It was a beautiful new building – it even had two halls, computer suites, two fields and a well-stocked library. On the surface of things we appeared to have it all, and yet I was not coping and I should have been. Looking back I can see that subconsciously I was *ashamed* that I was not coping well. I also felt *guilt* that as a result of my struggling I was letting other people down.

Subconscious solution? Avoid interactions with other people who might make negative judgements about me.

Hence, I was relatively comfortable interacting with the staff of a supermarket 15 miles away but could not risk a perceived further challenge to my self-esteem by someone who knew me closer to home.

It's a vicious circle, or in this case a vicious triangle!

What Chris was seeking to do was to be break the cycle at the point of avoidance. How? By graded exposure to the situations I was avoiding.

Graded exposure is a classic behavioural psychotherapy strategy for the treatment of phobias. Take someone who is suffering from agoraphobia, for example:

> 'Typically, a person with agoraphobia will describe a 'fear of fear', especially if they experience panics. They often avoid feared situations because they are afraid of bringing on a panic, not because the situation is inherently fearful.'

Dave Richards and Bob McDonald,
Behavioural Psychotherapy: A Handbook for Nurses

Treatment for phobias can begin with *visualisation* of the feared situation, for example talking with someone about the possibility of returning to work and the positive aspects of a return such as imagining being back in the confined area of the staffroom and being greeted by a few close colleagues who have missed you.

A short-term exposure to the visualised situation might then follow, accompanied by a close friend or family member.

An opportunity to reflect on and write down the positives of the experience might then lead to a longer exposure with more staff present and, for a class teacher, an opportunity to go down and meet and be greeted by their class for five minutes before break.

The key thing is slow exposure to the area of avoidance that builds into regular and sustained contact and desensitisation to the fear.

Most days I will walk Eddie, out for a walk in the countryside. He is a big dog, even for a retriever, and very strong. The exercise does us both good and I enjoy observing the changing of the seasons.

I usually take him out in the boot of my Mondeo estate. He will invariably come back filthy or wet, or preferably both (from his point of view). He is lying by my side right now looking at me through the corner of one eye, waiting for the cue for a walk and an extended swim in the Irish Sea (him, not me).

As a result of this he gives off an aroma of wet dog for much of the time. Couple this with his ability to shed his coat all year round, for the non-dog lover, I am not painting a particularly attractive picture.

My children are all grown up now, can drive, and have cars of their own and so rarely travel with me. On the odd occasion that they do, they always complain about how much the car stinks of dog. I am not aware that it does other than because they tell me so. The reason? Because I spend so much time travelling around the country in the car that I have become completely desensitised to the smell.

The desired end goal is that exposure to the fear leads to desensitisation that becomes habitual and embedded in our subconscious thinking. We become much more confident and self-reliant. It sounds easy on paper and it truly does work but requires practice and no short measure of courage.

Challenge

Are there any aspects of your professional life in which you subconsciously employ avoidance strategies?

If so, what do you do to avoid them?

Do you feel fear guilt or shame over them?

Why do you feel that way?

What could you do today to give you a limited exposure to the thing you fear?

How could you graduate that exposure over the next four weeks?

For some time, I had been avoiding people.

Shutting people out is like putting up an umbrella – it may protect us from the rain but we block out all the sunshine too. We need other people around us to confirm the positive aspects of our personality that we may have come to deny ourselves.

My comfort zone needed to expand beyond the house. Walking the dog and doing the supermarket shop had been important first steps, but I needed to expand my interactions. I began to see more of my wider family and friends; at home at first but then venturing further afield to other people's houses. They rarely spoke to me about school but seemed genuinely only interested in my well-being and my return to health. I had been off work for three months now. I was calmer, more rational and sleeping better – although all of these were comparative to the state I had been in.

Whilst I had been away, the school was being run by my deputy head and assistant head who were acting up. A mentor head from the LEA was also visiting to offer advice. I had had very little communication with school at all. I subsequently learned that staff and governors had been instructed that they were not to make contact. This was well intentioned and a good thing in many ways, although it probably added to my sense of isolation. A no-win situation.

The chair of governors came and visited on a few occasions and on one occasion brought the mentor head with them. They were very supportive. We largely skirted around talking about school except in relation to one ongoing issue that they were trying to gather documentation for. The LEA welfare officer also visited. She was kind and explained the need for me to be properly ready before attempting a phased return to work. She also took me through the various stages of the absence monitoring procedure and visits to occupational health. I have to admit that, whilst I appreciated the necessity for the process, that is exactly what it felt like – a process. When I did eventually return to work and had some time later to take someone else down the very same route I found it very difficult indeed. I wanted to give them a hug, not have a meeting with them and HR!

One other visitor was the Assistant Director of Children's Services with responsibility for schools. I was deeply touched that with over 400 schools he had taken time to come and visit me. We talked about a number of measures that could and would be put in place to support me on my return. Amongst these would be a review of how the school was funded to try and increase the non-contact time of the deputy and assistant head to assist in the running of such a large school.

A phased return was planned for the last six weeks of the academic year, but without me resuming overall control back from our deputy and assistant head who had done a fabulous job of running the school while I had been away. Instead, it enabled me to catch up on what had happened while I had been away. It also provided an opportunity for a graduated exposure to the environment that I had found so stressful. On the first visit I made it as far as my office, the second, the staffroom and on the third visit I walked down the corridors. Staff and children seemed so pleased to see me. Each visit became a little easier. I had two things I particularly wanted to achieve before the end of term.

- Firstly, one of the school's much admired and longest serving members of staff was retiring and I wanted to be able to pay tribute to the contribution she had made at her 'leaving do' with many staff, both past and present.
- Secondly, I wanted to be able to lead the Year 6 leavers' assembly in front of parents. I had missed so much of what was an important and special year for those children and I wanted to be able to at least give them a good send off.

Clearly, both of these were going to be big tests for me. Both involved the risk of stammering in public again and both exposed me to the risk of an audience who would inevitably be forming opinions based on my performance. My self-perceived success or failure was also high stakes for me, because with the six-week summer break, there would be plenty of time for me to ruminate for good or for worse.

I arrived for both occasions early. Chris has always advised me to arrive at events in plenty of time because our bodies can only maintain a surge of adrenaline for short periods. The longer we are in an environment, the more settled we become (it is of course the reason that it is never wise to arrive at an interview with five minutes to spare!). Working, as I do now, as a speaker and trainer, I like to make sure that I am set up a good 45 minutes before I am due to speak, to get that initial surge of adrenaline out of my system before speaking. I rarely read anything out in front of an audience, but I had written down what I wanted to say for both occasions, so that if I could not maintain my concentration and lost my way, I had something to refer to, to get me back on track.

I had another safety net. My predecessor had worked with the retiring member of staff for longer than I had. She knew of my predicament and graciously offered to step in if I lost my nerve either on the day or even during my speech. A senior member of staff also volunteered to do the same for the leavers' assembly. I was grateful to both of them. Knowing there is an available plan B can often make a huge difference in stressful situations.

On both occasions, my mouth was dry and there were beads of cold sweat on my forehead as I stood up to speak. There was a palpable sense of tension and anticipation in the room as I began.

So often in life, the anticipation is worse than the reality.

As I started to speak, falteringly at first, my confidence began to grow and the tension in the room began to dissipate. Neither were perfect performances – I stumbled a few times – but my stammer stayed largely at bay and I remained on the stage, referring to my script only the once.

One issue that needed to be addressed was that our deputy head would be going on maternity leave as I returned full-time in the autumn term. The governing body were very supportive and agreed to ask our assistant head, Wendy, to act up as co-head teacher with me for the duration of the deputy's absence (expected to be a year). This was an unusual move, but welcomed all round. These were somewhat less austere times and the LEA generously footed the bill. For the governors and local authority it also provided the stability of an acting head, in post, should I fail to make a good recovery. For me it was an opportunity to share, at least for a while, the running of this lovely but massive school. I felt no sense of ego around sharing the headship. I saw it as a really positive thing and a possible future way forward.

Without this level of support I am not sure how successful my return to work would have been. I am certainly aware that colleagues still had to cover for me and even protect me at times and I am hugely grateful to all those people who supported me through that time. Wendy, in particular, certainly dealt with some very difficult situations so that I did not have to.

There then came a golden opportunity for her to apply for a permanent headship of her own and so she left for this well-deserved promotion at the end of the spring term. The two terms working as co-heads were hugely rewarding, and I am grateful that we remain great friends to this day.

I had successfully made it back to school and the community I loved and continued successfully as a headteacher for five more years.

2006/2007 was my wake-up call. Whilst a few things did change at work and the LEA made good on their promise to review funding procedures, fundamentally I had started to recognise that the thing that most needed to change was me.

> 'If you want to know the person who is most responsible for where you are now, look in the mirror.'
>
> (Paul McGee, 2015)

I am not going to pretend that I always got it right from then on, or that I never suffered from stress again. However, I was able to resume my journey (something that had once seemed impossible). This time, I was more self-aware and better equipped with coping strategies. Many of these strategies were taught to me by Chris and I will share these with you throughout this book.

Take control. . .

Time management

People tend to become stressed when they feel out of control in a situation. There is much about working in education that is unpredictable so it pays to take control whenever you can – 'Control the controllable'. There are also many competing demands on our time, so working efficiently will help us to achieve more and give us a greater sense of achievement.

Good time management skills can make a significant contribution to reducing anxiety and stress.

- Preparation is key, so start well in advance with whatever task you are planning.
- Build in quick wins, however small, into large projects allowing everyone to feel that progress is being made towards the goal.
- Plan long term so that everyone knows the key priorities for each half term and where the 'pinch points' will be in terms of key tasks and deadlines.
- Set yourself clear deadlines. We are usually more focussed and productive when time is limited. Don't let tasks drift on.
- Have a master to do list and then daily ones broken down into 'must', 'should' and 'could'.
- Start each day by reviewing your list and by completing a short task that will allow you to get back into the work zone and give you an early sense of achievement.
- Keep lists of what you have done as well as what you plan to do.
- Be realistic about what you are likely to achieve each day. Work on the basis of five hours of 'planned' work. In education there will always be enough 'unplanned work' such as phone calls or visits from parents to fill the rest of the day. Over-scheduling your day can leave you feeling frustrated and reduce your sense of control.
- Give yourself short five-minute breaks during the day.
- Don't confuse working very long hours with working productively. They do not always equate.
- Getting things done is often better in the long run than achieving perfection. Sometimes 'OK' has to be good enough.

- Set yourself one or two nights a week to stay later and get through tasks with fewer distractions. Some people schedule that for Friday, so that they can take less work home over the weekend.
- Plan a regular no work evening at home, e.g. 'No work Wednesdays' to give yourself a proper break in the week to socialise, spend time with the family, or to pursue outside interests. Do not compromise on this.
- Accept that some days you will be more in the 'work zone' than others. It is human nature. Don't beat yourself up about it.
- A meeting mid-morning can break the morning in two – both parts too short to achieve anything substantial. Ditto the afternoon. Time spent in the lead up to a meeting can also be unproductive, so where possible, schedule meetings for either the start or end of the working day.
- There are times when you have to be politely assertive and say 'no' to people, particularly if saying 'yes' is likely to significantly impact on your ability to deliver on your 'must' and 'should do' tasks. Ultimately, you are not doing anyone any favours.
- 'If something can be done 80% as well by someone else, delegate.' – John C Maxwell (author).
- Try to reserve some time with no interruptions.
- Don't dwell on what happened yesterday, it won't change it. Concentrate instead on today and tomorrow.

Leadership interview

Chris Wheatley – Chief Executive, Flying High Trust, Nottinghamshire

Background

Chris believes that school leaders should have the moral purpose to accept the collective responsibility for improving the whole school system. This is at the heart of the vision of the Flying High Trust, firmly believing that collaboration is the key to successful school improvement and sustainability. At the centre of the trust is Cotgrave Candleby Lane Primary School, one of the first teaching schools in the UK. At the time of writing, the trust currently works with some 44 schools across a wide range of contexts to support school improvement.

Stressors

Chris and his team are at the forefront of finding creative solutions to school improvement in a constantly shifting educational landscape and the number of schools that they are supporting has expanded rapidly in the last two years. So what are the biggest stressors for someone leading a very different kind of organisation to anything that could have been envisioned ten years ago?

Chris told me that whilst he does experience the strong pressures of achievement targets, league tables and inspections, for him the greatest cause of stress is the vulnerability of the system itself. Although one of the first to embark on the teaching schools route, a flagship governmental policy, Chris describes their entrepreneurial approach as both operating without a blueprint and without a safety net. Chris advocates the need for new systems and organisations to be given the opportunity to embed themselves and not get caught up in political machinations but rather grow out of a position of trust.

Coping strategies

So how does he cope with that vulnerability and the uncertainty that goes with it? He relies on three factors:

1 Digging deep and drawing on all his reserves of resilience.
2 Remembering the moral purpose of what they are trying to achieve.
3 Being able to look himself in the eye in the mirror.

Outlets for Chris include jogging and/or twice-weekly visits to the gym. Whilst recognising that exercising is a great stress reliever, he also knows that sometimes he needs to be 'in that place' in order to get out there and exercise.

Managing stress in others

When things are particularly tough, Chris finds that the best method for managing stress in others is to remain and be seen to remain positive and reassuring himself.

> 'Reflecting positive thoughts back to people really helps.'

As the lead school in the trust, they pride themselves on their proactive approach to staff well-being. Staff are offered a massage on a Friday evening before leaving work so that they enter the weekend in a relaxed state. Acknowledging that everyone can have 'off times', there is a policy in place where two 'duvet days' a year are available as a recognition of 100 percent attendance or for staff who run extra-curricular activities. These days can be banked and taken into year two where a further two 'duvet days' are available. A further day in year three would effectively allow staff to earn a week's term-time leave.

Chris reports that this strategy works well and that absence levels due to work-related stress are low.

Advice to new headteachers or other senior leaders

> 'Find something that takes you away from school mentally.'

> 'Don't take yourself too seriously.'

> 'Don't live to work, we should work to live.'

> 'The key is to role model the behaviours that you would want from your staff. So make sure that you go to your own children's concerts, let people come in a little bit later on their kids' birthdays. Invest in people properly.'

Summary: Chapter 4

- When suffering from stress, anxiety or depression we often adopt learned helplessness and become victims of our own thinking.
- Wanting to change is an important first step in taking back control and thus in our overall recovery.
- We often find our comfort zone contracting dramatically making us risk-adverse. Finding ways to expand it again, with support, is very important.
- Big changes can seem very daunting. Small steps are far more manageable and lead to regular short-term successes.
- Guilt, shame and avoidance are often key contributors to mental illness.
- Graded exposure to the things that we fear helps to desensitise us to our stressors and helps to break the guilt–shame–avoidance cycle.

5 The enemy at the gates – Dealing with 'difficult' parents

There is only one way to avoid criticism: do nothing, say nothing and be nothing.

Aristotle

In Chapter 3, we learned that one of the top stressors for senior leaders was issues with parents. This is not surprising because it is an area we have far less direct influence over. Pupils' behaviour can of course be challenging, but we as staff are on hand and have a greater control over resolving matters – often nipping problems in the bud – so long as we know about them.

When a parent comes to call, the difficulty is that we will not have been party to the discussions at teatime the night before and we don't know what has been said, and in some instances the arrival of a parent at the door, or the letter dropped in at the school office, may be the first we know of an incident having taken place at all!

In such situations, much of the control is taken away from us and this heightens our sense of worry and anticipation. The situation is unpredictable and this can cause us stress. Of course this is part and parcel of the job, but when we feel that way for a good proportion of each working day it can have a lasting effect on our mental well-being.

I was no exception. As a headteacher, I often found that it was the unpredictability and volatility of relations with a small minority of parents that caused me the sleepless nights.

I want to state here, publicly, that the vast majority of parents that I have encountered in my career both as a class teacher and as a headteacher, have been decent people who have been very supportive of the schools in which I have worked. They also gave me a huge amount of personal support. They want the best for their child or children as any good parent would. I have also worked very closely with parents who have been governors and members of Parent Teachers and Friends Associations (PTFAs), who have worked hard and selflessly, not just for the benefit of their child but to support the school and local community. It is a testament to these people that many continue after their children have left the school or go on to offer their support in similar roles in secondary schools.

That said, it is universally recognised that, a small percentage of parents can take up a significant percentage of a head's time, proving a distraction from a plethora of tasks that need completing and acting as a significant stressor.

In my experience, parental responses tend to fall into one of the quadrants below.

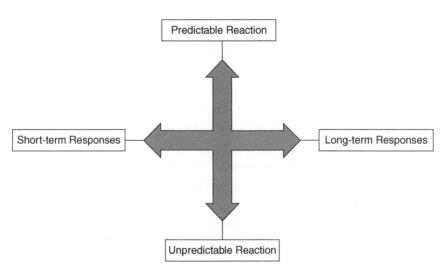

In my first headship, many of the issues with parents fell into the bottom left quadrant. They came out of left field and *could not* be foreseen. The response from the parent would often be volatile, unpleasant at the time, but relatively short-lived.

> **Example scenario**
>
> *A child misses coming in to the dining hall for lunch. He/she does not tell anyone in school but informs his/her mum when he/she gets home. Mum is angry and rings school to say it should have been picked up. By the next day she has had a chance to cool down and the issue is largely forgotten.*

Top left quadrant

Other issues *can* be anticipated and you know you will get a response. These fall into the top left hand quadrant.

> **Example scenario**
>
> *There are limited places for a school disco. A child brings money in for a ticket but the class is being covered by a supply teacher who forgets to send the money to the office. By the time the class teacher returns from absence and realises the error, it is too late and all the tickets have already sold out. A very angry letter is received from the child's dad on the day of the disco, demanding either a ticket or an apology. Again, not particularly pleasant to deal with at the time but once the error was spotted it was predictable that there would be some response from parents or carers. The response is likely to be relatively short-lived because beyond the date of the actual disco there is little that either party could do to alter the situation.*

Top right quadrant

Some responses from parents are entirely predictable, ongoing issues to be dealt with long term. These fall into the top right hand quadrant.

> **Example scenario**
>
> *I once had a parent who was fixated with the parking situation outside school. It was undeniably very difficult, as it is outside most schools. Where*

we disagreed, was that she thought that school staff should be trying to enforce the parking restrictions at the critical times of morning drop off and afternoon pick up. I did not believe that to be an appropriate action for staff to be undertaking. Nevertheless we did, at the request of the community police team, issue frequent reminders to parents via the school newsletter asking people to park considerately. More often than not it would elicit a response from the same parent restating their viewpoint. This went on for some years. It was a bit wearing at times, but it was predictable and the arguments were well rehearsed (on both sides!).

Bottom right quadrant

Finally, there is a fourth group of issues that fall into the bottom right quadrant where the timing of an incident and subsequent complaint is unpredictable but the consequent interactions with parents go on for weeks, months or sometimes years. For me, these were the incidents that caused me the most stress and distress.

Example scenario

Tommy (name changed), was a lovely lad in very many ways but experienced difficulties interacting with groups of children. He tended to have one special friend and would prefer to interact on a one-to-one situation at break time. This was OK, most of the time, until the friend wanted to go off and play football or was invited to play by another child. A classic case of two's company, three's a crowd would often ensue with Tommy often feeling pushed out and feeling upset. Rather than telling anyone in school, Tommy would go home and tell his mum who would get very upset and come into school the following day. Frequently the children would have made up by that point anyway and the situation would blow over for half a term or so when it would rear its head again. Again, Tommy would not tell anyone until he got home and his mum would have to deal with the emotional outpouring which in turn left her understandably distressed. Over time, the dreaded word 'bullying' began to be used. Staff did their best to respond and sort the situations out as we became aware of them and Tommy's mum was eventually pacified. There was no pattern to these fallings out. Weeks and months could

Tommy's dad's behaviour was designed to intimidate without any actual physical threat. Chris describes this kind of behaviour as passive aggressive. Long gaps between phone calls would leave me agitated and in fight or flight mode for extended periods, often taking in a weekend. This dragged on for several years, and it was the unpredictability of when it would blow up next and what the next response from the parents might be (e.g. a complaint to Ofsted and the implications of that) that caused the long-term stress.

Chris taught me to try and see the other side of the story.

'Try to understand Tommy's mum's situation.' Chris said to me one day. 'She wants, what any parent wants for their child, to be happy.' (I can't argue with that). 'Perhaps she is spending all day worrying if Tommy is having a good day and when he does get home and has had a bad one, he takes it out on her. She is frustrated that she is having to sort these things through, perhaps resulting in tea being delayed and Tommy taking a lot of coaxing to go to bed at night. Mum is tired when Tommy finally does get to sleep, collapses in the armchair with a glass of wine and calls Tommy's dad and recounts all that has happened in an emotional outpouring. Dad feels upset because mum and Tommy are distressed. His instinct is to want to protect them but he can't do that because he is away on business. He feels guilty for not being there and this guilt turns into frustration.' 'So,' says Chris, 'He rings you the next morning. He wants to vent his frustration and give someone a good verbal kicking. You are an easy target as the head of the school and so you get it, despite the fact that this might be the first you have heard of yesterday's incident. It isn't pleasant to deal with and may be harsh, but both the mum and the dad's behaviour is not really about you as a person. **It is not a personal attack on *you*.** If anybody else was sitting in your chair, *they* would be receiving the same phone call.'

Chris's approach admittedly involves a fair amount of conjecture, but it is a useful strategy on two levels.

1   This deduced story construct is more likely to help us empathise with the parents, increasing the possibility of an outcome that will satisfy everyone and preferably result in Tommy being happy in his friendships.
2   It is easier to deal with an unpleasant situation if we can rationalise other people's behaviour and realise that *they are upset or angry over a situation and not with us personally*.

When I think back over fifteen years of headship I can only think of a couple of occasions where parents actually had a problem with me personally, the rest of the time it was because I was the one sitting in the head's chair and the situation would probably have played out the same whoever had been sat there.

What Chris would also say about the above situation is that it is also about power play. Dad, however focussed he might be on Tommy and his wife's happiness, is feeling powerless. And so, Chris would argue, he tries to assert his authority by trying to dictate that a meeting should take place as well as its time and location and effectively the agenda.

'Your office, Monday morning, 9.00am to discuss what steps you have taken to resolve the situation to my satisfaction.'

Added to this is that I am also feeling powerless, because this is the first I have heard of the previous day's incident and because Tommy does not say anything to staff in school and so is not giving the school a chance to respond.

Therefore, I can agree to his dad's terms and conditions achieving a short-term appeasement, but I would surrender all control. In what other profession would you expect to be able to dictate the day and time of what is essentially a professional consultation? (You try ringing your local doctor's surgery and telling the receptionist that you demand to see your GP at 9.00 am on Monday morning, and see how you get on!).

Alternatively, I can take back some of the control over the situation and present my own terms:

'I would be very happy to meet you to discuss Tommy's unhappiness, but I would need to investigate what took place yesterday first. I do have a busy day on Monday but there is another meeting I could move to accommodate you, but I am afraid that will not be until 2.30pm.'

Reasonable and controlled, I demonstrate that I am trying to be accommodating and taking the issue seriously, but essentially taking back control. The more control I can take over a situation, the less anxiety I am likely to experience.

Another bottom right quadrant behaviour

Another bottom right quadrant behaviour can be characterised by what might best be described as 'the serial complainer'. These are the parents that you know are going to be a challenge all the way through their child's time through school but you really can't predict what they will get upset about or how they will react next.

The best example I can think of was in my first headship.

Example scenario

Hagrid, as he became known, was a giant of a man – bearded too! He and his three children, who were lovely kids, had done the rounds of the local schools and had finally ended up with us. (You know you are on a hiding to nothing when you are the last choice of school!) I was a new head with a new deputy, my (now) good friend Richard. Hagrid blew hot and cold with us. One day Richard might be in his good books and I was 'persona non grata' or vice versa. Some days we would both be in his good books and others he would be shouting in both of our faces. He had a mercurial temper that was completely unpredictable. He was capable of acts of great generosity donating expensive items to the Summer and Christmas Fayres; he also could present you with gifts with a rather more menacing undertone. I clearly remember the time he bought me an army surplus mirror on a swivel headed arm, the device used by the military to check underneath cars for incendiary devices. Generous gift or veiled threat? Who knows?

You could never be sure what Hagrid would explode about, but as well as the face-to-face encounters, he would often sit up through the night writing letters of complaint by hand which the children would then bring in on his behalf the following morning. One such letter concerned the perceived failure of the school to eradicate head lice from the pupil population as his children had, in common with many others, 'caught them' several times. The letter ran to fifteen pages of lined A4 and he had taped sample head lice that he had removed from their hair for my inspection. I kid you not!

Responding to his near daily letters over a range of topics including uniform, the Religious Education syllabus, end of year reports and voluntary contributions towards school visits, would take much of my morning. I came to dread the pre-school knock at the door and the handing over of another letter. I could feel myself get agitated as 8.50am came around.

Eventually, after many months of this, things came to a head (no pun intended). I cannot now remember what the latest issue was but it culminated in an invitation for both Richard and me to go to Hagrid's house. We knew that it was a somewhat risky strategy, but Richard is quite big and looks quite hard (he isn't) and we both felt that things could not continue in the same manner any longer. So we decided to accept the invitation and try to clear the air once and for all. We made sure that people knew where we were going.

We were there for hours. No sign of the children. The house was an Aladdin's cave full of gadgets and unidentifiable objects and contraptions. We were shown some children's dresses that he said had belonged to 'a princess'. For reasons of security, he could not tell us who they had belonged to but it was a princess who had been killed in a traffic accident (as far as I am aware that narrows it down to two people – so much for security!). Eventually we were taken outside to view the large garden and outhouses, being told to duck under the neck-high electrical cables which criss-crossed the plot of land. Touch them, we were told, and we would be electrocuted and certainly die. Really? Richard and I exchanged nervous glances as we followed him to the end of the garden which was hidden by a line of trees. He wanted to show us a sculpture. There was indeed a sculpture there, although it did seem a little strange to have a sculpture in a part of the garden that was not visible from the house, or indeed anyone else's house for that matter! However what was more odd and rather concerning, was that there were two freshly dug holes in the ground. They were roughly six feet in length, three feet wide and approximately five feet deep. Nothing was actually said and the three of us just stared at the two holes in silence. I glanced up at Richard and was instantly sure that we were thinking the same thing. Time for a sharp exit!

Honestly, you could not make this stuff up!

I cannot remember what excuse we offered for our speedy retreat – a made-up governors meeting perhaps. Nor can I remember how the conversation went around the issue that was the reason for our visit. I do not even remember the circumstances in which the family finally came to leave the school. I know Richard had left at that point to take up his own headship, but did the family leave the school first or did I? Who knows? But those holes, I have never forgotten!

I do remember that about a year after I started my second headship, I was in the main office when one of the staff answered the phone and told me that she had a gentleman by the name of Hagrid (he didn't actually call himself that, but you get what I mean) who would like to speak to me. I think the colour must have drained from my face as she quickly told me that she could tell him I was in a meeting if I wanted. What was the point of stalling from him I thought to myself – he's tracked you down! I was experiencing a real 'fight or flight' sensation as that phone call was put through, I can tell you.

I misjudged him. He had rung to tell me how well his kids were doing and to tell me that he was sorry that he had not had a chance to say goodbye to me when I left and that he hoped that I would do well in my new school.

I never heard from him again.

Whatever your role in school, the chances are that you will have had a parent who has got right under your skin. You will have your own tales you could tell and no doubt if you are experiencing that difficult relationship right now it will feel very immediate, very stressful and as if it will never end.

The purpose of telling you this story is threefold:

1   There are some parents for whom you will never be able to win and who are impossible to predict – so don't waste your energy trying.
2   My final phone call with Hagrid demonstrated, I hope, that he actually bore no real malice towards me personally, he just got very frustrated with a school system he did not fully understand and often didn't agree with.
3   Dealing with Hagrid was very stressful and felt very immediate at the time. The situation seemed like it would never ever end, but it did. All things come to an end – even the obstacles that other people can sometimes present in our lives.

In Ian Gilbert's book, *Little Owl's Book of Thinking: An Introduction to Thinking Skills* (2004), Benny the young owlet learns a number of woodland lessons from his wise father. One that particularly resonated with me was that even fallen tree trunks, that seem immense and block your path with no easy way around them, will eventually rot away.

The fact that there are now aspects of Hagrid's story that I cannot now remember is testament to that. And, there are other parents too, who have caused me stress over the years whose faces I can recall but whose names have slipped from memory.

No obstacle is forever.

Challenge

On the quadrant diagram on page 72, or draw your own on a separate piece of paper, try plotting on some of your more difficult relationships with parents. Use a circle to represent each parent, using larger circles for the relationships that cause you the most stress. You should then have a visual representation of the situations that cause you more or less stress at work.

One of my biggest issues when Chris first met me was that I had a tendency to catastrophise situations. By this I mean that I would worry incessantly about situations for which there was a good deal of uncertainty. When there was an absence of facts my subconscious mind would fill in the gaps and rehearse all the possible negative outcomes. I would then select the most negative outcome and prepare myself for that eventuality with heightened levels of anxiety.

Example scenario
Mrs Rogers (name changed) came to the office at 8.55am having dropped her daughter off after at the school gate and asked the office staff if she could see me before the end of school that afternoon. The office staff were really good at operating a triage system. With such a large school, we still tried to encourage an open door policy but actually not everyone who wanted to see the head actually needed to and would

sometimes be better signposted to someone who knew more about the question.

e.g. 'Can I ask what it is about?'

'It's about volunteering in school to help me gain some experience before applying for a GNVQ qualification in childcare.'

'In that case, you might be better having a word with Mrs Smith who deals with all our placements, she would be best placed to help you. Is that OK? Let me see when she is free. . .'

However on this occasion, Mrs Rogers said that she would rather discuss the matter with me personally. My diary was checked, an appointment was made for mid-afternoon, and I was made aware of the situation a short while later.

When her daughter had first started school our relationship had been very amicable. However, things had soured somewhat about eighteen months previously when a member of staff had made a mistake (who hasn't? and I won't go into it here) that had left the school vulnerable to criticism and necessitated me to apologise profusely.

The apology had been accepted by her parents, but a tension still hung in the air whenever we met.

Mrs Rogers was now asking for an appointment, but more than that, she would not say why it had to be with me. As the morning wore on, I began to imagine all sorts of reasons why. Had there been some repeat of the events of eighteen months ago? I found it increasingly difficult to concentrate as the day wore on and was not very productive all day. By the middle of the afternoon I had convinced myself that she had made a complaint to Ofsted.

My heart was thumping as I offered her a seat in my office and closed the door.

I braced myself.

It turned out that she had come to tell me that it was likely that they would be moving abroad with her husband's job. It wasn't certain yet and they didn't want to tell their daughter until it was. Hence, she had wanted to come before the end of school. She wanted to know a little about the transferring of school records when a child was moving abroad.

She also told me that notwithstanding the issue of eighteen months ago, they had been really very happy with the school and in many ways they did not want to leave.

I had completely misjudged the situation and, it seems, the parents. Perhaps any remaining awkwardness had been on my part. She had even told me that they had both really appreciated my apology for the previous events and my willingness to hold my hands up and admit that on that occasion, we had got it wrong.

I had also wasted the best part of a day worrying about a meeting that had actually been far more positive than I had imagined.

I engaged in this kind of thinking quite a lot over the years, and more often than not the meetings that I dreaded turned out much better than I anticipated. Looking back, I was probably more skilful at handling those difficult kinds of encounters than I gave myself credit for.

In one of our sessions, Chris suggested that I should divide a piece of paper into two columns. In the first column I listed as many meetings as I could remember where the end result had worked out better than I had anticipated. In the other column I listed all the situations that I could remember where the outcome was either what I had feared, or indeed worse. When I consciously thought about it, there were far more positive outcomes than negative ones.

Try it. . .

Challenge

Positive outcomes with parents	Negative outcomes with parents

Completing this exercise, and reviewing it regularly, helped me to get things into a little more perspective.

Try identifying some of the situations where the outcomes have been better than you predicted. This would not have come about by chance, so give yourself credit for the way you handled the situation.

Challenge

List the skills and strategies that you used to secure a positive outcome, such as giving parents plenty of time to speak, acknowledging their concerns, or making sure that you started and ended the meeting with a positive comment about their child.

Place the list somewhere where you can see it (but not clearly in sight of visitors), e.g. in front of your desk as a permanent reminder of how well you *do* handle awkward situations.

Although it was bottom right quadrant behaviour (long-term responses with a high level of unpredictably, see page 74) that caused me high levels of long-term stress, the bottom left quadrant behaviour (a short-term response that was unpredictable) also had a lasting impact on me. These are often characterised by angry encounters that seem to come out of nowhere. One example of this was when Molly's mum encountered me on the playground at the end of the day. Molly had come to school with an expensive new winter coat only to have the hood partially ripped off by another child as a result of some rough play. Molly's mum was fuming (which I can understand – new coats are expensive items). She was shouting at me, close up and in my face. 'The behaviour in this school has gone completely downhill! Aren't the children supervised at playtimes?'

This exchange took place in the full view and earshot of a good number of parents. I felt upset and embarrassed at being challenged in such a way. I managed to get her to come to my office, where and out of the public gaze I managed to calm her down somewhat. None-the-less, I struggled to get the image of her bawling at me out of my head for several weeks, particularly at times when my mind was less occupied, and when I was trying to get to sleep I could sense my elevated heart rate and quickening rate of breathing. If this sounds all too familiar to you, try this freeze-frame technique that Chris taught me.

Challenge

- Close your eyes.
- Picture the person or situation that is causing you stress.
- Freeze the image in your mind so that it becomes a photograph rather than a movie clip.
- Now imagine the colour gradually draining away from the image leaving you with a black and white photograph.
- Imagine the photograph gradually diminishing in size as it floats away to an imaginary horizon point and until it disappears.
- Now imagine a time, place or event at which you felt really happy and relaxed – a great holiday or a family wedding, perhaps.
- Visualise a colour photograph of this occasion appearing first as a pinprick on your horizon, and then moving slowly towards you, growing all the time until it occupies the whole of your vision.
- Start to slowly intensify the colours of the still image so that they become richer, warm and vivid.
- Unfreeze the image and allow it to play as a movie in your mind.
- Notice all the details you see, hear, smell, and feel.
- Draw up other positive movies in this way.

Looking back over my fifteen years of headship, it seems to me that the most successful and least stressful outcomes in difficult situations depend on three main factors:

1. Getting in there early

Things tend to gather momentum if not addressed quickly. Take the Russell Brand/Jonathan Ross radio show controversy of a few years ago. Listening figures for the actual live show itself were not stellar but people heard and read about it and a wave of righteous indignation began to grow even amongst people who had never heard what was said, but had read about it in the national press. I am not saying who was right and who was wrong but the BBC was slow to respond, allowing the issue to grow and grow.

When you are able to talk to parents about an incident *before* their child goes home and relays what will inevitably be a one-sided version of events, it can make a huge difference. This was of course the huge frustration of Tommy's situation – we didn't know!

2. Taking what control you can of the situation

I have already discussed this to a certain extent, but I would often find that when a parent booked an appointment, you could not be sure who would turn up with them. Sometimes they would come alone, or they might bring their partner as well or a grandparent of the child or a friend. I even had a situation once where a parent had booked an appointment and brought three other parents with them who felt strongly on the same issue. I was outnumbered and outgunned!

Where the issue was known, and where plausibly relevant, I liked to bring another member of the SLT in with me – preferably somebody who had existing positive relationships with the parents and/or the child.

Not telling parents that I was doing so beforehand meant that I was asserting my control over the meeting. My office – my meeting. However, I would always ask courteously: 'I hope you don't mind but I have asked Mr Jones to come and join us because he has a really good relationship with Kirsty and has been really pleased with her progress this year.' Some people may have been taken aback by this a little, but I never knew a parent to say 'No'!

Where possible, I would try and contrive the seating arrangements to work like this:

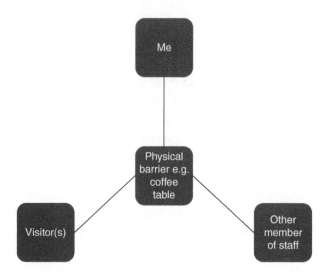

This was usually easy to do with gestures of the hand: 'Please sit down and thank you for coming.' This arrangement has clear advantages:

- There are two people to listen to, recall and respond to whatever concern or argument is being put forward – reducing the feeling that it all lies on your shoulders and therefore reducing your level of anxiety.
- The most confrontational situations involve direct eye contact. That is more difficult when there is another member of staff in the room, particularly if they are not in the direct eyeline of your visitor.

Asking parents if they mind if you take notes also works well. Again, it means that you are not in extended eye contact with them, but also people tend to be more cautious about what they are saying if they know it is being recorded in some way and particularly in front of someone else!

3. Taking some of the heat out of the situation

- Thank them for coming in at the start and end of the encounter.
- Emphasise that we all want to do what is best for their child.
- Start and end with positives about their child.
- Listen and listen some more. Trying to construct counterarguments when they are in mid flow will only inflame the situation. This way, you have more time

to collect your thoughts and respond in a reasoned manner, staying calm and professional whatever the provocation. Given the chance to have their full say, I have known parents to even apologise for coming in in such a cross manner.

- I always tried to include an apology somewhere. People do like to hear the word 'sorry'. That does not mean to say that you are necessarily accepting their viewpoint, or that the school or a member of staff was necessarily in the wrong. Often, 'I can see you are really upset about this and I am truly sorry that you felt you had to come in' will suffice.

- Don't try to cover the inexcusable. If you, or someone else on the staff has made a mistake, admit it and apologise. Like in the case of Mrs Rogers, people will respect you more for it in the long run.

- Make sure you summarise at the end of the meeting what actions the school and, if appropriate, the parents will be taking as a result of this meeting, however small. People on both sides of any situation are always looking to see what they can take away from a meeting. Always give them something.

Take control . . .

Relaxation

Relaxation is very important in our lives, as it helps to relieve the symptoms of stress and consequently improves our health. Many people in education work very long hours, and whilst acknowledging that the holidays are a real plus of the job, they often do not give enough time for themselves during term time. This can have a negative impact on memory as well as having the potential to lead to mental and physical health problems. It's important to build in at least ten minutes relaxation every day in order to unwind. This could be something as simple as soaking in a hot bath, going to the gym or relaxation exercises. We are all different, the important thing is to find something that works for you and keep doing it. As with most things, we get better with practice.

If school leaders want their staff to remain resilient, they need to be seen to be clearly modelling these behaviours themselves rather than modelling a 'work till you drop' approach. (see the 'Take control' sections on breathing (page 28), mindfulness (page 166) and sleep (page 48).

- Relaxation techniques will not make worries and anxieties disappear, but you will feel more able to deal with them when you have released the tensions in your muscles and cleared your thoughts.

- Many relaxation techniques combine deep breathing with muscle relaxation. Yoga and t'ai chi are both good forms of exercise that can help to improve breathing and relaxation.

- Some people find that alternative therapies such as massage, acupuncture, reflexology and hypnosis help them to achieve a more relaxed state.

- When anxious, many people experience an almost subconscious tension in the muscles around the neck and shoulders. For a quick muscle relaxation technique in your office or classroom, lasting no more than three or four minutes, try the following:
  - Try raising your shoulders up as far as you can and holding for three seconds before releasing. Repeat three times.
  - Let your head drop forward on to your chest. Slowly rotate your neck anticlockwise at its full extension towards your left shoulder,

round to your back, towards your right shoulder and finally back to your chest. Repeat three times.

- With you fingertips, seek out any knots, or tender points in the muscles in your neck and shoulders and apply pressure and hold for several seconds before working the fingertip out away from the point of tension.
- Practise breathing deeply from your diaphragm, breathing in through the nose, holding the breath for three seconds and exhaling through the mouth.

If you don't have three or four minutes, try applying aspects of these exercises through the day and you will experience the benefits.

- Use laughter as therapy. It is well known that when we laugh the brain releases endorphins which acts as a sedative as well as reducing our perception of pain. Finding a stand-up comedian, or television programme that makes us laugh, is very therapeutic. The ability to find humour in situations and not take ourselves too seriously, can also help to give us perspective.
- The physical health benefits of exercise are well known but the mental health benefits are becoming more appreciated. Exercise is a very effective way of countering the effects of stress. It too, boosts the production of endorphins that make us calmer. Many people report feeling more relaxed and focussed after a short run, workout or aerobics session. Even walking at a vigorous pace can help us to feel better.
- Music has the power to transform our mood. Construct playlists of soothing music. If you feel yourself getting anxious, try a little classical music to calm you. Music that has a tempo of 60 beats per minute connects with the human heartbeat. It slows down the heart and rate of breathing, helping you to relax. Alternatively, try listening to a playlist of songs that will help transport you to happy memories and good times.
- Try taking your mind off your troubles by visualising a place where you would feel safe and calm, such as a sandy beach or a woodland scene. Imagine in detail what you can see, hear and smell. The more detail the better.
- Relaxation skills are exactly that. They are skills and the more you practise them, the more effective they become. So, don't be hard on yourself and think that you're not doing it right or it will potentially become another stressor.

Leadership interview

Ava Sturridge-Packer CBE – Executive Headteacher, St.Mary's Teaching Alliance, Handsworth, Birmingham

Background

Ava was appointed as headteacher of what is now St. Mary's CE Primary and Nursery Academy 19 years ago, taking on what was then a failing school with a substantial deficit budget. Ava turned the school's fortunes around and St Mary's is now a teaching school. In 2011, Ava also became Executive Head of the nearby, struggling St. Michael's CE Primary. The Birmingham Anglican Diocese is the sponsor for St. Michael's with St. Mary's as the partner school for school-to-school improvement. In 2014, St. Michael's (now an academy) achieved Ofsted judgements of 'Good' across the board. St. Mary's currently has 350 pupils on roll and St Michael's 170.

Stressors

For Ava, overall workload, governance, behaviour, changes in national policy, league tables, parent issues, Ofsted inspections and staffing issues can all be stressors at different times.

> 'Parent issues, can be very stressful at times but they are not a consistent pressure. They tend to come and go in phases.'

> 'Ofsted inspections are by their very nature highly pressurised, but the main stress is the unpredictability of the personalities of the team. Not everyone can engage with everyone successfully. Will they get it? Will they get your vision for your school and what you are trying to achieve?'

However, Ava says that her greatest source of stress is resolving staffing issues.

> 'It can be very challenging and takes up a lot of thinking time and resources as the potential consequences for the organisation are huge. Even with SATS results you feel a sense of control – we do the right things and standards will rise. But with staffing issues, there are so many variables and threads. It is very complex.'

> 'The one thing I don't tend to worry about any more is the budget. I inherited a £90,000 deficit and we were in Special Measures, things have never been that bad again. We had to improve but not spend any money.'

Coping strategies

Ava is part of a large and close-knit family unit. Spending time with them and talking things through with them allows her to step back and maintain a sense of perspective – a good sense of humour helps too. She has a strong Christian faith and says that at extreme times, that has made the difference and given her the strength to get through.

'I tend to pray more when things get tough. Faith helps me to believe that things will get sorted and that there is always a bigger picture.'

Ava has always loved to dance and has taken part in many different styles of dance but actually finds that just dancing in her own front room helps her to unwind.

'I find it hard to immerse myself in a book, but I do enjoy watching films with a moral purpose where somebody overcomes adversity.'

Managing stress in others

'I actually find trying to help other people with their stress levels helps me manage my own – it gives me a sense of perspective.'

Ava emphasises the importance of finding *quality* time to *really* listen to staff.

'However busy you may be, snatched conversations will not truly help. It's OK to say, "I am really busy at the moment, but you are more important." I try to help people see through their problems and offer some practical strategies. "So what can we do about it to help you?"'

'It is important to keep in mind that situations in someone's home life can impact on work and vice versa. You often cannot give them the solution but you can buy them thinking time. Sometimes allowing the member of staff a couple of days off allows them to start to think through, but you need to emphasise that whatever they are going through you still need them to deliver in the classroom.'

Both of the schools that Ava leads buy into an external package for staff support for any kind of stress including bereavement.

Advice to new headteachers or other senior leaders

- Be aware of what you can affect and what you cannot.
- When things get tough, get back to the classroom and refocus on what really matters.

- Remember, particularly in an age of social media, you are always public property.
- Take time to be kind to yourself and take time to be kind to other people.

'I expect a lot, so I try to give a lot – you need to make staff feel that they are real and important. If staff have their own kids' sports days – I let them go. If it's their kids' birthdays, I let them go early. If they are caring for elderly parents who have medical appointments I let them go. I would far rather people were honest with me. Compassion is so important.'

Summary: Chapter 5

- Dealing with issues with parents can be a significant stressor for school leaders.
- Interactions with parents can be long term or short term, predictable or unpredictable.
- Each combination of the above will cause varying levels of anxiety for different people.
- Maintaining as much control as we can over a situation reduces our anxiety, increases our confidence and is therefore more likely to lead to a positive outcome.
- Trying to understand people's motivations can help both increase our empathy and depersonalise the situation.
- Some people's behaviour is completely unpredictable. Accept that, and don't waste your energy trying to predict it.
- No obstacle lasts forever.
- Try to avoid catastrophising, concentrate instead on the positive outcomes you have secured in the past and the skills and strategies you used to secure them.
- Freeze-frame techniques can help you to block out unwelcome thoughts and memories.
- Simple strategies can help to dissipate aggressive behaviour and take the heat out of situations.

6 The enemy within – Dealing with 'tricky' staffing situations

No one can make you feel inferior without your consent.

Eleanor Roosevelt

In the last chapter, we examined some of the ways in which external pressures on a school can cause us stress and suggested some strategies to manage the anxiety we might experience. Nothing lasts forever, not even difficult parents, Ofsted inspectors or Secretaries of State!

Sometimes, we find ourselves in relationships that can cause us to feel stressed.

> **Example scenario**
>
> A few years ago, I knew a teacher called Polly. Polly was generally the life and soul of the party and had a wide circle of friends who she socialised with.

However, she had one close friend, Sharon, a dental practice manager who she would often moan about when she got to work. Polly would usually see Sharon two or three times a month, but over the last couple of years it had increasingly been Polly that was having to pick up the phone to arrange a meetup. But although it was Polly that had made the call, Sharon would invariably dictate where they should meet. Polly was finding this increasingly annoying, and coupled with this Sharon would often arrive very late. Polly could feel a churning sensation in her stomach each time that this happened and would often return home feeling very irritable.

Things came to something of a head when one Friday evening Sharon cancelled a get-together with some rather unconvincing excuse that Polly did not fully believe. Worse than that, the phone call to cancel came just half an hour before they were due to meet. Polly had had another invitation to go to the cinema that night but had turned it down because of the existing arrangement with Sharon. It was now too late to go to the cinema and, in any event, Polly was concerned that it might just look like she was tagging along because she had no better offer on the table.

Polly spent the evening in with a bottle of wine but couldn't shake the agitated, negative feelings that she was experiencing. 'Why am I doing this?' she asked herself. 'I am the one doing all the chasing and yet Sharon is dictating her own terms on our friendship. She cannot value my friendship highly for her to treat me in this manner and yet I keep coming back for more.'

Polly finally came to the conclusion that Sharon was exerting complete control over their relationship and decided that she really did not need any added stress in her life thank you.

At this point Polly took back control. There was no great bust up but she decided to limit the stress that Sharon was causing her by seeing her far less often.

Sharon now sometimes calls her.

It is generally a good idea to cut out relationships that lead us to feel stressed or knock our confidence and damage our self-esteem, just as Polly did. It is relatively easy to do that in our social lives, but far harder to do that in school. As a headteacher or senior leader, you might well appoint like-minded individuals as vacancies come up. You will almost certainly be looking for people who will support your vision for the school and from whom a certain degree of loyalty will be a given – you gave them the job they wanted after all! However, unless you are opening a brand new school, there will always be some colleagues that you will have no choice but to work with. (It is worth remembering that most staff in school get no choice at all!)

Schools would be incredibly dull environments for children to learn in, if all staff had similar personalities, but it is inevitable that there will be some colleagues that we find more difficult to work with than others. If we find them in some way a threat to our own situation, those relationships can become quite stressful and damaging over prolonged periods of time. Relying on those people moving on is not a great coping strategy – some staff will stay in the same school for their entire career.

It can be particularly difficult in a small school if you have a difficult relationship with a member of staff. If your school only has three teachers and you don't get on with one of the other teachers there really are very few places to hide!

Although, on one occasion, I was seconded to work as acting head of a small village primary, both of my substantive headships have been in very large schools which gave me some flexibility as a head in where I placed people. For the most part, we were able to put together year group teams with people who were likely to work well together. Where we had personalities that just did not work as well together, we were able to place them in different year groups. Sometimes that would even entail them being in a completely different building! Apart from at the weekly staff meeting, they could have as much or as little to do with one another as they wished.

Inevitably, as a head or senior leader in a school you are not afforded the luxury of separation. You have to work with everyone, try to get on with everyone and get the best out of everyone.

Some years ago, and before I met and worked with Chris Roome, I worked with a teacher called Joanne (name changed). Joanne was a member of the Senior Management Team (SMT) as it was called back then until someone, somewhere, decided that Senior 'Leadership' Team sounded more proactive: 'We don't just draw up playground rotas you know!'

Joanne was older than me, and after several quick promotions early on in her career things seem to have stalled and plateaued for her. I was a young headteacher and Joanne had not been my appointment.

She had a searching stare that made me feel rather uncomfortable – as if she was reading my mind and finding it a rather short read! I often sensed disdain as if she felt that that she could do my job rather better than I did.

She sometimes gave me withering looks, for example, when I dressed up as Professor Dumbledore from Harry Potter. (Be careful about dressing up – in one school I worked in, the male staff had to come dressed as women and vice versa. This was for Comic Relief, I should add. My car broke down on the way to work. All very embarrassing.)

Joanne was a popular member of staff with the year group team that she led. They saw her as championing their cause, which she did, often very effectively. You see Joanne was highly articulate and when she chose to, she could deconstruct other people's viewpoints very effectively and put forward a well-constructed counterargument. Joanne seemed to have a view on everything which she was happy to share in both SMT meetings and in our weekly whole-school staff meetings. The problem was that many people felt quite intimidated by her and often sensed that if they engaged in an argument they would be likely to lose, publicly. Pitched arguments between senior leaders in staff meetings are never a good idea, and even after I would clear my throat and cordially say, 'Perhaps we could park that issue for now and discuss it at the next Senior Management Team meeting', this was usually met by an uneasy silence and with Joanne's last remarks and opinion remaining hanging in the air.

What made matters worse was that she was never on time for SMT meetings and she would always try and block any new ideas that I was putting forward.

Increasingly I would begin to dread both staff and SMT and feel myself getting agitated as each one approached at the end of the teaching day.

I am, of course, being desperately unfair to Joanne on two counts: I have given only my biased and one-sided account of a fellow professional who I struggled to get on with at times; secondly, I have given Joanne no right of reply, so I have changed her name instead. Whilst this all took place some years ago now, I recently decided to review this difficult relationship as, aside from taking a member of staff through a disciplinary procedure (which is never going to win you friends), this remains one of the most stressful relationships I have experienced with a colleague.

So looking back, is there anything I would have done differently? Absolutely!

- Firstly, in admitting that perhaps there were things I could have done differently, I am accepting some responsibility, which at the time I found really difficult. Back then, I felt it was Joanne's fault for being the kind of person she was. Full stop. In reality, I should have acknowledged that it takes two to make an argument, as my Grandma used to tell me whenever I had fallen out with one of my siblings.

- I now recognise that I was actually quite intimidated by Joanne at times and worried about the fact that she held such sway with people. As I have told you before, one of my failings is that I worry too much about what people think of me. Perhaps my own insecurities were fuelling my actions, turning the issue, in my mind, into some kind of a popularity contest. I don't think I ever really stopped to try and understand Joanne's motivations at the time. Perhaps she was intimidated by me? Perhaps she harboured resentment because her own career had stalled? Was there something I could have given her as a professional development opportunity that might have made her feel that things were getting back on track? Possibly, if I had tried to understand her motivations a little better I might have avoided some of the bruising encounters that left me (and possibly her) feeling stressed.
- Thirdly, I don't think I chose all my battles terribly wisely, which made our relationship quite adversarial at times.

You don't have to win every encounter in order to win the war.

When we are stressed, anxious or depressed we tend to use generalisations as currency. The truth of the matter is that Joanne was *sometimes* late for meetings, rather than *never* on time. She also did not *always* try and block new ideas, she *sometimes* did. I did once tell her that she was *always* late for meetings. It was neither helpful nor accurate and it did little to improve the situation or our relationship. It was also a statement that could be easily disproved.

When we deal in generalisations, we are in danger of making matters personal and risk 'playing the player and not the ball'. Looking back, a better approach would have been to talk to her quietly and in private.

'Joanne, I couldn't help noticing that you were late for the meeting tonight. I get frustrated when people arrive late for SMT meetings because we often end up going back over early items on the agenda, which is not a good use of everyone else's time.'

Speaking to her in those terms would have depersonalised the issue. It was a behaviour I was unhappy with, not her as a person. It is really just a more sophisticated version of the message that we often give to children who have been in trouble: 'I like you Lucy. I think that you are a great kid . . . *but* that does not mean I always like the way you behave and I do get upset when you. . .'

Most people respect fairness and my more reasoned, retrospective approach to Joanne's timekeeping might have started a new and more positive view of me rather than just reinforcing the negative view she already had.

By stating my feelings ('I get frustrated when. . .'), I would also have kept matters within the realm of fact rather than opinion. I would also have shown that I was accepting some ownership of the situation, making it less confrontational.

Challenge

Think of a situation where you have had a difficult encounter with a colleague.
What did they do that left you feeling angry or upset?

What might have been their motivation for the way they acted?

Was there anything that you said or did that might have worsened the situation?

Imagine you are going to revisit this encounter. Without avoiding the issue all together, what could *you* do differently to try to bring about a more positive outcome for both parties.

Replay the scene in your mind as you would hope it would now play out.

I have always been a little impulsive, preferring to wade right in when a little more forethought and planning would serve me better. (You should see me with an IKEA flat-pack!) As you will have gathered by now, I found issues hanging over me very stressful at times. When discussing dealing with issues with parents I shared the advice of getting in there early, however, I soon learned as a head, that the opposite was often true when dealing with issues.

Tackling a situation with a member of staff when either or both people are still feeling worked up is not always a great idea. While that adrenaline is still surging and our hearts are furiously pumping oxygenated blood to our limbs, we are truly prepared for fight or flight. Neither scenario is likely to result in a positive outcome. People will often become either very defensive or go on the attack, and things may well get said in the heat of the moment that are not entirely professional. Once they are out there you cannot unsay them.

Waiting until the next day before re-engaging with the situation allows us to do a number of things:

1   reflect more calmly on the situation
2   make sure we consider the situation fairly and ensure that we tackle the behaviour rather than the person
3   rehearse our response
4   avoid 'kitchen sinking' (see below).

Kitchen sinking

In his book, *Stress Management for* Dummies, Allen Elkin describes 'kitchen sinking' as:

> *'What you do when you lump a bunch of grievances together and throw them at the other person all at once.'* (Allen Elkin, 2013)

For example:

> *'and I didn't have your literacy planning in last week, your class cloakroom is a mess and I have noticed that you have consistently used practice with a 'c' throughout your end-of-term reports when the verb, which I presume you meant to use, is spelt practise with an 's'!*

It is very easy to slip into this way of talking sometimes, particularly if you share your house with teenagers and when our tolerance levels are low. You will probably find that a few parents will behave in this manner at parents' evening! However, it can and does come over as grasping at straws and you are again likely to push the other person into a corner.

Looking back at my time working with Joanne, my generalisations of her behaviour: 'She's always doing this' or, 'she never does that', blinded me to some of her good qualities that I now recognise, but failed to appreciate at the time. She was, for example, really hot on discipline around the school and making sure that the children maintained the standards of politeness and behaviour that we expected. She was a particularly good teacher of maths, and she was generally very good at sorting out issues with parents. I believe that she also had the children's best interests at heart, and that counts for a lot.

Challenge

Think of a colleague (either past or present) that you have sometimes had a difficult relationship with which has caused you stress.

Write down three behaviours they engaged in that you found difficult to cope with. (This should be easy!)

1

2

3

Now try to think of five positive qualities about the person.
Come on, you can do it . . . Really you can!

1

2

3

4

5

There, that wasn't so bad was it?

Exercises like the above can help us to put perceived difficult working relationships back into some kind of perspective.

In all fairness to Joanne, if we had a difficult relationship, *I* was part of the problem. Because she *sometimes* (not always!) acted as a blocker to new ideas that I wanted to push through, I was not very good at listening to her. 'Oh here she goes again!' would say the voice inside my head and the mental shutters would come down until she paused for breath and then I would be straight back in there.

When I think back, all the really great heads I have known and worked for, have been great listeners – all of them!

I had pretty much stopped listening to Joanne because I didn't want to hear what she had to say. Because I had become blinkered to any of her good qualities, I had very little that I could offer her in the way of positive feedback about her work. So, if I were to place myself in her shoes, I would guess that she probably felt that her opinions were not welcome, that I did not value her and that I did not have anything good to say about her. When a professional, or actually any other relationship, ends up like this it results in what Chris Johnstone describes as, 'A vicious cycle that maintains and amplifies conflict.'

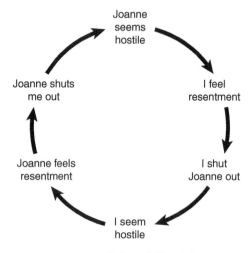

(Adapted) Chris Johnstone, *Find Your Power* (2010)

I can now see that one of us really needed to break this vicious circle, and I think that should have been *me*.

Active listening and acknowledgement of Joanne's concerns would have cost nothing and did not mean that I had to agree with her. Statements like, 'Thank you, you have raised some valid points and concerns there; having considered what you have said I am still of the view that. . .' would not have surrendered my control, but would have made Joanne feel that her views were being listened to and valued if not actually agreed with!

Similarly, making myself complete an exercise such as the one above would have helped to ensure that I would say something positive to her at least once a week, such as, 'I really appreciated you handled that situation with Mrs Grey yesterday. It can't have been easy, but I thought you diffused the situation brilliantly'.

Just by doing these small things I could have broken the cycle of resentment. Actually, as the senior leader, it was *my* responsibility to.

It is human nature to want to surround ourselves with people who make us feel good about ourselves and affirm our positive qualities. I was recently running an 'Art of Being Brilliant' session for my friend and colleague, Andy Cope. It was an in-service training day for a cluster of schools and I asked them to consider a question that Andy often poses:

'If you could be a superhero for a day, who would you be and what would your special powers be?'

A lady's hand shot up immediately and she said: 'That's easy, I would be Mind-control woman – then everyone would think like me!'

It's an appealing prospect isn't it? Think how short staff meetings would be for a start! Also, no one would get anxious about Ofsted because the lead inspector would always be on our wavelength and tell us what a fine job we are all doing!

Truthfully, surrounding ourselves with people who are going to agree with everything we say is a risky strategy. What if, in a moment of madness, you decided to bet all Class 7's trip money on the horses at the 2.30 at Newmarket? Wouldn't you want someone to scream *'Don't do it!'*?

Although my working relationship with Joanne was not always easy, her tendency to question things did save my skin on more than one occasion, such as the time that a newsletter was sent to classes to go out that night and she spotted a sensitive piece of staffing information that had been included that had not yet been through the board of governors. All the newsletters had to be reprinted, but it was a small price to pay against the difficult and embarrassing fallout that could have ensued.

It is also true to say that *sometimes* Joanne's forthright views would provoke a discussion that would refine and improve an original idea that had been put forward.

It would seem true that you sometimes need a little grit inside the oyster shell in order to produce a pearl.

One of the biggest stressors in my early days as a head was actually caused by me. I set myself the unrealistic expectation of always having to have the answer. This of course relied on me knowing everything, which clearly I do not. Consequently, when a member of staff posed a difficult question in a staff or leadership meeting or expected an instant decision, I would get visibly flustered.

Many years ago, I was seconded to the LEA to deliver training for the new Science National Curriculum. It was in the days when an original, full subject set of subject folders would have filled your living room.

It was my first experience of acting as a trainer, and as young teacher I was feeling pretty daunted at the prospect of standing up in front of groups of teachers who had, in many cases, been doing the job for years. Remember, this was the first time that the curriculum had been prescribed, and many teachers were unhappy about it and felt that it was a challenge to their professionalism. And then this 'young whippersnapper' who had only been teaching for five minutes was going to get up and tell them how to teach primary science. So yes, I was excited by the opportunity, but was also experiencing some trepidation. There were a number of us being seconded to deliver English, maths and science training across the authority and on our last preparation day we were all gathered together and given a pep talk by a very senior figure within the LEA. What he actually delivered was an inspiring hour's session full of hints and tips on leading courses, based on his many years of experience. There was a question and answer session at the end and I put my hand up and enquired, 'What happens if someone asks me a question and I don't know the answer?'

He gave the following reply. 'You smile at them confidently and say: "That is a really good question, I wonder what the other people in the room think?"'

It was great advice and it came back to me years later when as a head I was posed a challenging question in a staff or leadership team meeting. 'I wonder what other people in the room think? It would at the very least buy me a few moments thinking time or, given the opportunity, somebody else would come up with a brilliant answer that I had not thought of.

As a leader, expecting yourself to have all the answers is unrealistic and places you under an enormous amount of pressure.

As a leader, you don't have to have all the answers, often the answers are out there in the room.

I now run courses and workshops on stress management and resilience for a living, but even now someone will occasionally ask me a question that will completely flummox me. I smile at them confidently and say, 'What do other people in the room think?'

What strategies do you use, or have seen other people use, to buy time when under pressure for an immediate response or decision?

I was talking to a headteacher recently who had to lead a staff meeting in which some difficult messages would need to be delivered. I asked her what her strategy was going to be. She told me that such meetings were a bit like a game of draughts. There were too many variables to be able to predict the exact outcome of a game. However, in draughts you can meticulously plan your first few moves. If you can get those to play out the way you intended, you stand a much better chance of winning the game.

It struck me as a very sound analogy. We all experience levels of anxiety when delivering difficult or unwelcome messages in schools. Planning the first steps of a meeting in meticulous detail allows us to feel more in control of the situation, reduces the anxiety we might be experiencing and affords us the best chance of the meeting playing out in the way that we want.

Delivering difficult messages usually goes hand in hand with changes ahead. How well staff react will often depend on their subconscious assessment of whether the changes exceed their own perceptions of their ability to deliver. If the demands seem unobtainable, their stress levels will increase (and possibly yours as well!).

In his book, *Find Your Power*, Chris Johnstone references studies of mythology carried out by Joseph Campbell. Many great stories involve a journey of some description – a geographical journey, or perhaps an emotional one, or both. A recurring theme is that the journey starts with some kind of 'call to adventure'. Take JRR Tolkien's, *The Hobbit,* for instance. (I loved this book as a child.) Bilbo Baggins has no thought of changing his lifestyle or his ways but he is visited by Gandalf, the grey wizard and Thorin's band of treasure-seeking dwarves. Bilbo finds himself gradually sucked into their 'call to adventure', to reclaim their lost gold from under the watchful gaze of Smaug, the dragon. Finally he can resist their vision no longer and joins their quest. Crucially though,

Bilbo sees a clear role for himself in the adventure – that of burglar. A role that none of the rest of the group can perform. They experience many set-backs and periods of doubt, but are always refocused by their mission, their 'call to adventure'.

How often do we as school leaders sell a vision of a journey, a call to adventure, where everyone feels they have a role to play and that role is valued?

Or do we sometimes, inadvertently, tell people that they are going on a route march with no clear destination, no end in sight and on which some will fall by the wayside if they don't keep up?

The ability to sell a vision to staff is highly important in helping them manage their reaction to changes ahead as well as their (and your!) levels of stress. But, however well we might sell a change, idea or vision, there will always be some people who will respond to the notion negatively. They will present you a million and one reasons why it is not desirable or practicable. If they have been in the profession a long time, they may well point out that it has been tried before, it is nothing new and that it didn't work last time and it won't work now!

This is difficult enough when done publicly in a meeting as Joanne was sometimes inclined to do, but even harder when you suspect it is happening behind your back! Dealing with the known is often hard, but dealing with the unknown is even trickier. A friend of mine who has recently become a deputy head in a secondary school has noticed for the first time that people go quiet when he enters the room and that some conversations are clearly no longer for his ears! Whilst it is easy to slip into paranoia and worry too much about what other people may be saying, negative thinking can be catching and a barrier to real progress.

In his book, *The Naked Leader* (2002), David Taylor refers to people who behave in this way as 'negs'.

> *'The disciples of doom have had it their way for too long – it is time to stop them. Involve and encourage them – if they don't play ball then take them on. Just leaving them to one side does not work.' (David Taylor, The Naked Leader)*

What really struck me about this was the point that people who he describes as 'negs' or perhaps another term could be 'blockers', thrive on telling other people that you do not listen to them or ask their opinion. Ignoring them is actually playing right into their hands and giving them more negative ammunition to use. Dealing with such individuals can be draining, damaging and at times stressful.

So much of stress management is to do with taking back control from the person or situation that is causing us the stress. So how do you take back control from someone who claims they are never listened to? David advocates approaching the 'neg' in an informal situation, but whilst with a group of other people, e.g. during coffee break in the staffroom, or at lunch (when you are not patrolling the dining room!). Next, make some idle chat involving the whole group before bringing up a subject that you know that the 'neg' has a particular interest in or involvement in as part of their role in school. Then invite the 'neg' for their thoughts on the subject. Everybody can see you asking for and listening to their opinion so the notion that you never seek their views is publicly dismantled.

'It is brilliant, because they cannot announce that they have no thoughts! I have done this many times and many "negs" have turned around and complained about me to my face, which is exactly what I was seeking.' David Taylor, The Naked Leader

Taylor goes on to point out that 'negs' who rise to power often become bullies who seek to control the thinking of others who are intimidated by them. However, bullies and 'negs' are also often people who are desperate to feel valued.

Challenge

Bring to mind someone you regard as a 'neg' or blocker.
   Try to think of three things you could do to make them feel as if their opinion matters to you and that they are valued and appreciated.

1

2

3

As a leader, how good are you at saying 'no'?

I strongly suspect that for many people the answer will be 'not very'! The inability to say 'no' is something that is not confined to school leaders – most people who work in education find it very difficult to say. Why? Because the vast majority of people are passionate about making a difference to children's lives and that often means going above and beyond. Most people who saw teaching as a convenient 8.30am to 3.30pm job have long since left the profession once faced with the ever-increasing demands on their evenings and weekends. The notion of contracted hours is laughably absurd to most people in the profession, and I have yet to meet anyone who actually believes that their job description accurately reflects the functions they perform – teacher, mentor, actor, parent, social worker, nurse and whipping boy for society's ills. We care passionately and that is why we sometimes take on too much for our own good!

Saying 'no' isn't being selfish. Sometimes when you say 'no', you are honouring your existing obligations and ensuring that you can be able to devote the time to them that they deserve.

Some schools develop a culture of 'upward loading' – essentially when no one wishes to, or feels empowered to solve a particular problem or concern, it gets passed on through year group or subject leaders (for those schools large enough to have them – I was once seconded as Acting Head of a four-teacher school in serious weaknesses – no such luxury!) up through senior leadership until eventually it lands firmly in the lap of the head. It is not great for staff development if they feel they have no responsibility for finding solutions, but it also puts incredible pressure on senior leaders to find all the solutions. I sometimes used to say to members of my SLT, 'Don't just bring me a problem, bring me at least one possible solution', and actually the best (and quickest to be promoted) did. The very best are now headteachers themselves.

However, it is important to develop the ability to say 'no' without feeling guilty, because taking on too much will increase our own levels of stress. We only have a finite amount of attention that we can give. Taking on more and more only dilutes the attention that we can give to each issue or challenge and we can end up doing none of them terribly well. Our professional pride then causes us to feel guilty creating further pressure on ourselves.

We are usually the best judges of how many plates we currently have spinning. Sometimes taking on something additional that we then fail to deliver on, is far worse than actually saying 'no' in the first place. It is reminiscent of the parable from the Bible of a farmer who asks his two sons to help in the fields. One says, 'Of course' but fails to appear. The other says, 'No!' but later appears to do the work. The son that said, 'Yes' but then failed to deliver let his father down more by the expectation he had created. Equally, by taking on the spinning of one extra plate, we risk smashing at least some of the ones we have spinning already.

To try to create the illusion that we somehow have limitless capacity does no one any good – least of all ourselves!

Many of us find the word 'no' very direct and abrupt, which as 'people' people makes us uncomfortable. There are other ways of refusing which say the same thing less directly.

> For example, a member of staff asks you for help but you are up to your neck in other issues.
>
> **Direct approach:** 'No, I can't.'
>
> **Indirect approach:** 'I would like to help you out, but I really can't.'
>
> The latter response maintains the same position but is softened and shows you do care.

As a head of a very large primary school, I often used to find myself 'hijacked' in a very well-meant way, by parents who had strong and often personal attachments to a variety of charities that did great work. The parents would often ask if we would do a fund-raiser in school. In the ideal world I would have said 'yes' to every request because they were all great causes. In reality, it would have meant us doing four or five such events per half term which would have led to complaints from other parents about fundraising overload.

I hated saying 'no' particularly when I was caught on the hoof face-to-face. I got much better at saying: 'Clearly we would love to because it is such a great cause, but I would need to have a look at the school calendar and see what else we have got on as we do get such a lot of requests.' It was a far more gentle let-down for them when, having collected my thoughts and having looked at the diary, I got back to them and explained that we really had got too much on as a school at the moment and that I hoped that they would understand. They usually did.

Stalling strategies often give us the space to accurately assess whether we have the time, mental capacity (and desire!) to take on something new. Examine your obligations and priorities before making any new commitments. Ask yourself if this new commitment is important to you. If it's something you are passionate about then go ahead, if not, then don't. Sleeping on it is often sound advice.

If you *are* going to say 'no' though, be honest as to your reasons. Don't fabricate them (as much as anything it is more to have to remember!) and don't give too much detail – you can appear overly apologetic.

Be prepared too, to say 'no' more than once; some people can be very persistent and if they sense a guilt chink in your armour, they will exploit it. Politely and calmly repeat your original rationale for refusal.

Take control...

Anger and tolerance

Anger is a normal, healthy emotion and we all experience it to some degree, often as a result of a perceived injustice against us either at work or at home. Bottling anger up is like shaking up a bottle of fizzy drink but keeping the cap on the bottle – you know it will all come out at some point, and when it does it's going to be messy! Many people bottle up their frustration at work because of the possible consequences of an outburst, but then find that their tolerance limits at home are limited and relatively small issues, such as a child of their own failing to tidy their room, can become a trigger for a disproportionate response. Disproportionate venting of anger and frustration both at work and home is likely to have consequences which in themselves can bring about more stress. It is better to manage anger, as uncontrolled anger can take a toll on both our relationships and health.

- Be aware of what is likely to trigger your anger and have a plan of how you will respond when you feel the anger building in you.
- Avoid reacting, or making decisions when you know you are angry. Give yourself space and, if possible, sleep on it.
- Take a deep breath and count to ten. It is easy in the heat of the moment to say something you'll later regret. Take a few moments to gather your thoughts before saying anything — this also allows anyone else involved to do the same thing, and reduces the chances of the situation escalating.
- Use deep breathing techniques (see Take control – Breathing (page 28)) to calm yourself.
- Visualise a relaxing scene such as walking on the beach and picture yourself being calm there.
- Depersonalise the trigger for your anger by tackling the behaviour rather than the person.
- Take ownership of your anger and frustration by using 'I' statements, such as, 'I get upset when you arrive late for meetings' rather than, 'You're always late!'
- Avoid 'kitchen sinking', e.g. saying, 'And another thing, while we are at it!'

- Be assertive rather than confrontational, stating your concerns clearly but without winding up the other party.
- Be aware of using non-confrontational body language, e.g. avoid clenched fists and folded arms.
- Be respectful.
- Be prepared to actively listen to the other person to gain understanding.
- Miscommunication and misconceptions are the cause of many conflicts. Ask questions to clarify that your perceptions of the situation are correct, e.g. 'Am I right in thinking that. . .?'
- Think what you would like to happen moving forward.
- Trying to identify possible solutions to the situation is both a constructive way through anger and helps to make you feel more in control.
- Ask yourself what you can do to improve the situation.
- Don't hold a grudge. Retained anger after the event is destructive to the emotional well-being of all concerned.
- Be prepared to apologise for your part. An apology is not necessarily an admission that you were wrong, rather a signal that your relationship with the other party is more important than being seen to be right.

Leadership interview

Ash Venkatesh – Headteacher, Littleover Community School, Derby

Background

Littleover Community School is a large, high-performing comprehensive school on the southern outskirts of the city of Derby. There are currently 1,760 pupils on roll. Ash Venkatesh is in his fifth year as headteacher of the school, having previously served there as deputy head for a number of years.

Stressors

Ash feels very fortunate to have a large team of staff that he can trust and that deal effectively with many of the curriculum and pastoral issues that inevitably come up in such a large school. They ensure that the issues that arrive at his door are the ones that he really needs to be dealing with. Consequently, whilst many heads of smaller schools have to worry about a myriad of issues such as a leaking flat roof, the leadership structure of the school allows for other people to pick up and deal with many of the issues that crop up.

A bigger pressure for him, is to maintain the school's excellent academic record.

> 'The school has had a strong academic reputation over many years and so people, including the media, tend to be very alert to small deviations in results. There is also the associated concern of maintaining the school's "Outstanding'" Ofsted judgement.'

These are matters that Ash takes very personally and so some of his pressures are ones that he places upon himself.

Coping strategies

> 'It is really important to talk to other colleagues on the Senior Leadership Team (there are seven in total). Problems thus become shared problems. As a member of the SLT, you sign up to this to some degree but it is really to make sure that other staff are able to concentrate on the core task of teaching.'

Before becoming a head, Ash says that he found it relatively easy to unwind in the evenings or at weekends – just watching television would help. As a head, it became harder and he would often find his mind returning to issues at work that he was dealing with.

Taking up evening classes in Italian has proved a good way of unwinding – keeping the mind challenged and occupied, not only in the classes themselves, but also when practising during the week.

> 'For a while I neglected my personal fitness, but now I try and visit the gym once or twice a week. I usually plug my earphones in and listen to podcasts while I exercise. I now feel fitter, healthier and more energised at work.'

Managing stress in others

Ash emphasises the importance of being available to staff and listening to their worries as well as role modelling that behaviour to other leaders.

> 'Inevitably, as Head, not everyone will want to come and talk to you but you do tend to end up dealing with the more serious issues with longer-lasting implications.'

> 'It's not so much about workload and longer hours – we all experience them. What it is about is engagement, that the work you do is productive and having a sense of satisfaction that you are having an impact.'

> 'You cannot always solve people's problems for them, and how you approach a situation depends not only on the role they are in, but what they are prepared to accept.'

Ash recognises that with people within the profession often starting leadership roles younger and working longer, it is becoming increasingly common for people to ask to reduce to working four days a week later in their career. As a school, they are generally amenable to that idea provided that:

- people understand the implication of the reduction of income to themselves
- there are some teaching and learning responsibility enhancements that need to be covered by full-time staff, and people recognise the implications of this.

Advice to new headteachers or other senior leaders

'Have and maintain outside interests.'

'Family and friends are often an important stabilising influence. Make sure that you have people both in and out of work to talk to.'

'Set limits to your time spent working. It is not a job like any other, but it is still a job and not your whole life – you can only do things to the best of your ability.'

'Try not to challenge yourself in all aspects of your role simultaneously.'

'Don't be in a rush to progress your career – careers will go on for longer now and there is an attraction to being well-established in a role. Pace yourself.'

Summary: Chapter 6

- Where possible, minimise the influence of people who cause you stress.
- As a leader, if you are not part of the solution, you are part of the problem. Choose your battles wisely.
- Tackle behaviours and not personalities. Avoid 'kitchen sinking'.
- Listen, listen, listen.
- Try not to respond to issues when you are fuelled with adrenaline. Sleep on it whenever you can so you can rehearse responses.
- Sell change as a call to adventure, not a route march, and reconnect people with the vision frequently.
- Beware of 'upward-loading'.
- You know your limits – stick within them and don't be afraid to say 'no'.

7 Two-dimensional thinking in a three-dimensional world? – Handling the pressures of inspection

Bravery is not the absence of fear but the forging ahead despite being afraid.
Robert Liparulo

Being a school leader is in many ways one of the best jobs in the world – a chance to help individual children achieve their potential, prepare them for an uncertain world of exponential change and, in no small way, help to shape a future generation. It is a privileged position and can be very rewarding.

However, there is nothing quite like a phone call from Ofsted announcing their intended visit to drain the colour from a headteacher's face (or any other teacher's for that matter) and to set their heart racing.

Along with issues with parents, one of the greatest causes of work-related stress amongst education professionals at all levels is down to the pressures of external accountabilities such as Ofsted and HMI inspections. This is somewhat ironic, as Sir Michael Wilshaw, the current head of Ofsted, seems to be of the view that teachers don't know what stress is (as noted in the introduction).

Perhaps he needs to spend more time in schools, or given that educationalists are the third most high risk occupation for work-related stress in the UK (see chapter 2, page 32), he should instead spend more time with GPs or therapists like Chris, who report the rise in the number of teachers that are referred to them.

The direct and indirect pressures of an inspection are the most commonly identified stressors amongst all the headteachers that I have interviewed and spoken to in the course of writing this book. They were also among the top stressors for headteachers in our survey of one hundred education leaders (see chapter 3, page 45).

Whilst, over time and a long career in teaching, many individual days have slipped from memory, I remember with clarity each and every day of the four inspections that took place in schools where I was headteacher. My abiding, retained emotion is one of frustration.

I remember the frustration of my first inspection as a headteacher, in an era of inspection where staff were issued summary grades of their observed lessons at the end of the visit. This was a supposedly confidential process between the teacher, the inspection team and the headteacher. We had three members of staff with the same surname but different initials. Despite wearing name badges with these initials clearly displayed, each of these three teachers received grades for subject lessons that they had not been observed teaching and in some cases belonged to a teacher in an entirely different key stage.

I remember with equal frustration being told in my final inspection, that not *all* our Reception children were making progress in a certain 20-minute period. Many had been in school less than a week and were still having to be enticed from their mother's side, having their tears wiped, learning where to hang their coat and how to sit on a carpet in a circle. And they weren't all making progress in that 20-minute period. *Really?* I felt for both staff and children.

My experiences are not unique, most heads and senior leaders will have similar tales to tell and will I am sure, have experienced that sense of frustration at some point, when either inspection teams simply get things wrong or the process that they are following defies logic and what we as professionals understand about how children learn, e.g. a sobbing four or five year old is not likely to make good progress during 20 minutes.

'Find me a wall and I will happily bang my head against it!'

I have yet to come across a headteacher who does not believe that schools should be accountable for the education they provide. When I first started teaching 30 years ago (ouch! – is it really that long) there were a few teachers

I encountered who saw it as an 8.30am to 3.30pm job with an hour's lunch break and good holidays. There were even one or two of whom you might have questioned whether they actually liked children at all! But such have been the spiralling expectations and workload of the job that these people left long ago. Who in the modern profession did not join in order to make a positive difference to children's lives? Children only get one shot at an education and so schools should be ambitious for their children and always be striving to improve.

So, if we accept all of the above, why is an Ofsted inspection such a stressful experience?

The more in control we feel of our lives, the less stress we feel.

The Ofsted inspection

1. An Ofsted inspection is the ultimate uncontrollable

We have no control over the timing. I know headteachers who anticipate inspections. Under the current system they build themselves up to a Wednesday lunch time, knowing that if they have not received 'the call' by that point 'They' will not be coming that week, only to start the build-up again the following Monday.

We also have no control over who comes to visit. It is like taking in a group of lodgers you have never met before. Whatever Ofsted might tell us about how the process is uniform, and however they might tweak and tighten up the inspection framework and judgement criteria, I still believe that so much rides on the personalities of the inspection team, and in particular that of the Lead Inspector. I am sure that most school leaders (though probably not Sir Michael Wilshaw) would agree.

It is common sense. Schools are made up of human beings and we all interact in different ways. Over the years I am sure that I have interviewed several hundred applicants for teaching and support posts. It has been suggested, that when interviewing we make up our minds about a candidate in the first five minutes and then spend the remaining 25 minutes looking for things that will justify our opinion. Whilst I have met many decent, open-minded inspectors, I have sadly also met those that give the impression that they made up their mind in those first five minutes. This may either be within the first five minutes of having arrived in the school, or even within the first five minutes of looking at the school's data.

You will not dissuade me from the view that much rests on the personalities of the team.

2. The goalposts keep moving

Having effectively planned and carried out improvements to address points from their last inspection, schools, unless they are already graded as 'outstanding'*, will be aspiring to achieve at least the next highest grade in their subsequent inspection. To then find that there has been another change to the framework or evaluation schedule, which then jeopardises that grading can be deeply unhelpful.

Similarly, if you *are* an 'outstanding' school but a new schedule threatens that judgement, this can also be a very stressful position to be in. The situation can be further exacerbated if you have little time to make alterations before an impending inspection (a school is a little bit like an oil tanker – you cannot change direction in an instant). It would be a little like the exam boards changing the A level syllabus six weeks before the exam and expecting pupils to pass papers based on the new syllabus. There would be a public outcry and some very stressed students, I suspect!

*If all schools achieved the top grade of 'outstanding', surely they would not stand out. They would be average surely – or am I missing something?

3. The stakes have never been higher

For many of the headteachers that I have interviewed, the pressure lies not so much within the inspection process itself as with the potential fallout if things do not go as well as planned. The damage to a school's reputation can take a long time to repair and the local press can be less than kind in their reporting. Headlines such as the following, ranging from the milder end of the spectrum to the more extreme end, are common:

(Name) School criticised by Ofsted Inspectors

Local schools' reputations take a hammering from Ofsted

Crisis hit (Name) School slammed again by Ofsted

'If things are not going very well, for any reason, it is often very public and quick to be seized upon by parents and the media. There is a tendency to reflect more on failures and disappointments than on successes.'

Dr Peter Blunsdon

At the time of writing, *The Guardian* has just published an announcement by Nicky Morgan, the Secretary of State for Education, under a newly elected, all Conservative government that:

> **'Headteachers at "coasting" schools could be sacked under new plans to improve failing institutions, it has been announced.'**
>
> *'The move, in a bill due to be introduced in the Queen's speech, could potentially affect hundreds of schools in England.*
>
> *Schools that are not considered to be performing as well as they could be will be put on an immediate notice to improve. They face having their leadership replaced, being taken over and turned into an academy if they fail to come up with a clear improvement plan.'*
>
> The Guardian, May 2015

This, combined with no offering of a definition of what constitutes a 'coasting school', will do little to calm the nerves of heads and other senior leaders and typifies the kinds of pressures that bear upon the profession. Uncertainty, inevitably, leads to stress.

4. Everyone is stressed at the same time!

An inspection is probably the only time in school when all members of staff are stressed at the same time. This is particularly difficult for heads and senior leaders as they are trying to keep everybody else calm, positive and focussed, whilst managing their own stress levels at the same time. It's a tall order. When we received the call several months after my return to work, I felt the colour drain away from my face and I felt sick to the pit of my stomach.

Do not make the mistake of believing that the pressure of facing a common stressor such as an inspection will necessarily bond people together. Every person's stress is different. If you experience an unfavourable inspection outcome as a senior leader it might mean more school improvement planning, more frequent governors meetings, dealing with uncomfortable questions from parents and the press, as well as a lovely long chat with one of Her Majesty's Inspectorate of schools. An unfavourable outcome as a class teacher might mean greater levels of scrutiny including planning, marking, monitoring of your pupil's work, displays, adherence to school policies and increased lesson observations. All of which will almost certainly lead to increased working hours and a shift in work/life balance.

Being aware of the different nature of stressors for different people within a school can help leaders to more effectively manage the pressures experienced by other staff as well as themselves.

What three things do you most fear about the outcome of your next inspection?

-

-

-

What three things would other members of the SLT most fear about the outcome of your next inspection?

-

-

-

What three things would classroom teachers most fear about the outcome of your next inspection?

-

-

-

What three things would support staff most fear about the outcome of your next inspection?

-

-

-

The time leading up to an inspection can be crucial in terms of shaping staff's thinking and mindset.

What could you do in advance of the inspection to address some of those fears?

So, if we cannot eliminate the stress of the inspection process, what can we do to minimise it?

It would be arrogant and disingenuous of me to suggest that I have all the answers to the levels of stress that an inspection can bring. Besides, if I had all the solutions I would be writing this overlooking the Mediterranean rather than the Irish Sea! I have experienced the pressures of four Ofsted inspections and one HMI visit in my time as a headteacher. I will be honest, and say that with constantly shifting expectations, these were amongst the most stressful times in my professional career. So, aside from the general advice offered on managing stress both in yourself and others that appears throughout this book, I draw upon the collective wisdom of all the headteachers I have interviewed to offer the following advice in terms of Ofsted:

*Whilst there is much about the process that is beyond your control, it pays to prepare well and... **control the controllable.***

- David Bateson
  'Knowledge is power, so know how you are going to be judged – understand the latest framework and guidance. It is a test of how well you know your school so be robust in your knowledge of what you are good at and what you need to improve upon.'

- Ash Venkatesh
  'Do your background research thoroughly. However hard you prepare, the process will be scary but scary and mysterious is a very challenging combination. Try to take the mystery out of it by really clueing up on the process and what it is likely to bring – that at least is within your control.'

- **Sue Goodall**

  Sue Goodall suggests that we should not make the mistake of thinking that we should know it all.

  'You don't and can't – its constantly changing. Don't be afraid to draw on other people for practical advice either.'

- **Jane Rutherford**

  This is echoed by Jane Rutherford, as head of a secondary school many times the size of Sue's village primary.

  'Make sure you have the right people available to go into the right meetings – as a head of a large school you cannot know everything.'

Most of our heads emphasised the importance of knowing your data inside out, particularly the story behind any dips in attainment. Be clear in your own mind about what is working well and what is not.

- **Wendy Rose**

  'It pays to know your shortcomings and be able to readily talk about what you have put in place to address them as well as the impact of those measures. Where you know you may have an issue tease out what is good within that area. For example, if pupil progress measures within a particular year group are not good try and identify a sub-group such as disadvantaged pupils, where progress is good.'

- **Peter Blunsdon**

  Peter Blunsdon also emphasises that you need to be prepared to justify your position and rehearse doing so before the inspection.

To whatever extent a visit from Ofsted may be expected, or not, that initial phone call can leave headteachers feeling on the back foot. Knowing the first steps you are going to take once that phone call comes will help you to feel more in control of the situation.

- **Jane Rutherford**

  'It helps to have a clear, written plan of who does what the moment the phone call comes. Having a clear procedure helps to maintain a clear focus and keeps people calm. It removes some of the unknowns.'

Plan your first ten actions following receipt of notification of inspection.

1

2

3

4

5

6

7

8

9

10

Now share these with your SLT, the wider staff and governors.

Managing staff stress during an inspection

Very high levels of anxiety amongst staff are not going to allow them to approach the inspection with a positive mindset. Absence of information fuels stress levels and people tend to fill in any void in communication with speculation. Try to minimise this by communicating in an effective and open manner.

- Many of our heads stressed the importance of making sure that staff are well briefed on the process ahead, so that there is no mystery in it. Make sure somebody in a senior position, who understands the process well, is available to answer any questions.
- Ensure that all staff know the school's key identified areas for development and what steps are being taken to achieve them.

Both of the above are good practice but try to do them *well in advance of any inspection*. Having to learn and retain a lot of information at very short notice will only increase the stress levels of the staff and distract them from their core task of delivering great lessons during the inspection itself.

Worries such as 'What if _____ goes off on one when I am being observed?' are common and are again an unwelcome distraction from what you want people to be really concentrating on.

Where there are 'known unknowns', such as a pupil or parent that might kick off during an inspection, have a plan in place in advance of the inspection of who will deal with it. You may well have to depart from that plan during the inspection, but the very fact that such a plan exists will calm the nerves of class teachers who may otherwise have to deal with the issue.

> *'Don't tell staff, "They can take us as they find us!" This is your opportunity to show your school in the very best light, so know the things that you are absolutely not going to let them leave your school without seeing. Staff need to see you being in charge.'*
>
> *David Bateson*

Without causing panic, all staff need to avoid complacency, particularly if working in schools previously graded as 'good' or 'outstanding'. Ava Sturridge-Packer, a trained Ofsted inspector, as well as a head, emphasises this.

> *'Never be complacent, inspection frameworks are changing all the time and schools that might have been judged as 'good' five years ago would not receive that judgement now.'*

The vast majority of staff want to make a positive impression during the inspection process. Indeed, having worked for most of my career in large primaries, I have known some teachers who have not been seen at all during the inspection (sometimes because they are part-time). Rather than feeling relieved, many experience a sense of anticlimax or even guilt, that they have not been through the experience in the same way as other colleagues.

Headteachers and SENCOs get a very tough time at the moment, and it may feel to a few members of staff as if the success of any inspection is down to them. It is imperative that all staff realise that, whilst some will spend more time with the inspectors than others, they all have an important contribution to make.

> *'The senior leadership team get a tough old time in schools.'*

'It is so important for staff concerns to be heard and dealt with, but we need to support our senior leaders to deal with the issues and not set them up for failure. Discuss issues openly and respectfully and offer solutions. Everyone in the school has the power to change things and we need to work together to do so.'

(Sarah Findlater, *How to Survive an Ofsted Inspection,* 2015)

Good teamwork is vital to the inspection process, but is not something that can be turned on at the flick of a switch. It is built on trust and part of the culture of the school. Like a garden at the Chelsea flower show it needs constant attention.

Whether staff like it or not, the inspectors are indeed coming and there is little to be gained by being anything other than welcoming, pleasant and co-operative.

To stay strong, staff need praise, reassurance and to feel appreciated.

Give credit where credit is due. Most staff will put in many extra hours before the inspectors arrive. Despite the nerves you yourself will be feeling, don't forget to thank them on the morning of the first day of the inspection. Equally, despite the exhaustion you will all be feeling, gather the staff (preferably for a free glass of wine!) and thank and praise them, regardless of the final outcome. If things have not gone as well as you hoped, discourage any talk of blame.

Managing your stress during an inspection

Tempting though it is to work through burning the midnight oil the night before the inspection, arriving in school thoroughly exhausted will make the process even more stressful. Trying to relax the night before is rather a tall order, but trying to find some form of mental distraction for an hour the evening before the inspection is helpful, if possible.

Realistically, you are not going to get a very sound night's sleep the night before, but many people lie awake worried that they may either oversleep or that the alarm will fail to go off.

Making sure that you have a backup alarm such as on your mobile phone, will reduce that anxiety and give you a better chance of getting some sleep.

If you don't already do it, put a pad of paper and a pen by your bedside. If something important occurs to you in the night you can then write it down. Trying to make sure you remember something in the morning is bound to keep you awake. For further advice, see Take control – Sleep (page 48).

On the morning of the inspection make sure you have a substantial breakfast. You probably won't feel much like eating, but remember that you don't know when you will next get a chance to eat and working on an empty stomach will not aid your concentration. In the ideal world, you should have a meal in the middle of the day but realistically that may not be possible, so take a supply of slow energy release foods such as bananas, blueberries and nuts that you can grab when you do get a moment. For further advice, see Take control – Nutrition (page 188).

It is highly likely that you will experience a build-up of muscular tension during the course of the inspection, particularly in your shoulders. This in turn can lead to the unwelcome distraction of headaches. To avoid this:

1 Try raising your shoulders up as far as you can and hold for three seconds before releasing.
2 Let your head drop forward on to your chest. Slowly rotate your neck anticlockwise at its full extension, towards your left shoulder, round to your back, towards your right shoulder and finally back to your chest.
3 With your fingertips, seek out any knots or tender points in the muscles in your neck and shoulders, apply pressure and hold for several seconds before working the fingertip out away from the point of tension.

Finding time during an inspection is always difficult, but these techniques take seconds and will help to dissipate any built-up tension. For further advice, see Take control – Relaxation (page 88).

Most inspections will afford you some moments of doubt or uncertainty. At such times take a moment to practise controlled breathing. Pause for a moment and make sure that you are breathing from the diaphragm and not your chest.

1 Inhale through your nose counting in your head to three.
2 Hold the breath for three seconds before exhaling through the mouth while counting for a further three seconds.
3 Repeat.

Controlling your breathing in this manner will help to steady you, leaving you feeling less tense and more in control. For further advice see the section entitled Take control – Breathing (page 28).

Strong leadership during an inspection

Lead the inspection from the outset and sell the inspectors your story and your vision for the school.

Ava Sturridge-Packer believes that stress is contagious in schools and that as a headteacher or senior leader you can stress others by your own stress.

> 'When the Ofsted call comes, if you become a headless chicken staff will start to stress. They are looking to their leader for reassurance. You need to appear confident however quickly your heart might be racing.'

Write yourself a 50 word affirmatory statement, e.g. 'I am a highly-dedicated, child-centred professional with a proven track record in raising standards.'

Learn that statement. Look at yourself in the mirror in the bathroom and say the statement out loud if you ever start to doubt yourself. (It might be as well to check that there is not an inspector in the next cubicle. This actually happened to me once.)

> 'Have a plan of who and what you want inspectors to see in what order. You will most likely have to deviate from it, but it is still a pathway that you aim to return to and follow. Be consistent in what you say. Be pleasantly assertive and don't be bullied. They are guests in your school. If you have concerns about the tone or approach of the team, do not be afraid to record conversations or ask for other people to be in meetings with you and record so that you have more than one set of ears.'

David Bateson

Sue Goodall emphasises the need to be prepared for surprises.

> 'It will never go exactly as you expect and whatever the outcome it is only two days out of your life.'

However well an inspection might go, there are still likely to be aspects of the judgements made that you will disagree with.

> 'Sometimes inspection judgements are not accurate reflections of what you know about your school. This is so hard, but you know your school best and have to stay true to what you believe. But actually, beyond all of this, the best preparation is to make teaching and learning your primary focus on a daily basis.'

Jane Rutherford

I recently met Derbyshire cricket captain, Wayne Madsen. In 2012, in his first season as captain, Madsen led a young Derbyshire side to the LV County Championship Division Two title; their first trophy since 1993.

It struck me that as Captain, Wayne must have to contend with decisions from an umpire that he may view as incorrect and that potentially could affect the outcome of a match. Seeking a different perspective, I asked Wayne how he copes when a decision with high stakes goes against his team and an injustice occurs.

Wayne emphasised the need to stay in the here and now and not let your mind project forward the consequences of that decision. He stated that whilst he might go over to the umpire and ask what he thought of the ball that had just been bowled and the rationale behind the decision, if an opposition batsman had not been given 'out', for example, his priority had to be to refocus the bowler and 'get them back on the horse'. This is not always easy, particularly if that batsman then goes on to score highly.

> 'You cannot allow yourself to be distracted by the umpire's decision. You have to think about it later because if you dwell on it, it will affect the overall performance of the team and you will let other opportunities slip by.'
>
> Wayne Madsen

Wayne also emphasised the need for the captain to have someone to vent any frustrations to during the match, usually the coach. Having someone to offload to allows him, as captain, to stay focussed, because if he cannot let a decision go and move on then he risks compromising the whole match.

It strikes me that leaders in school could take from this and that it would be a good idea for heads to find a trusted colleague in another school that they can ring, however briefly, during the inspection process and know that that call will be answered, giving that opportunity to offload and refocus.

Don't try to cover up underperformance of a member of staff. Ultimately you are not doing them, the school, or yourself any favours. Let the team know you have concerns and make sure you have a clear support plan in place, with time-related targets.

> 'Be brave. Don't be afraid to take them on. You know your school, so make sure that you show it to them. Don't let external factors drag you down or make you feel insecure.'
>
> Chris Wheatley

Throughout the process, be honest and true to yourself and what you believe in. Don't live a lie. You will not be happy with yourself for doing so even if the report is good – besides which you run the risk of being caught out. These 'house guests' are trained to look for chinks in your armour and sniff out inconsistencies. If they find them, that is neither good for you nor the school.

'To see what is right and not do it, is the want of courage.'

Confucius

Take control . . .

Confidence

People's levels of self-confidence vary enormously, but most people, I believe, would confess to wishing to be more confident than they already are. When we feel confident, we feel far more resilient and able to deal with the stresses and strains of everyday life. Whilst events in life can set our confidence back, there are also concrete actions that can be taken that help to boost confidence and self-belief. As C.S. Lewis put it, 'We are what we believe we are.'

- To be confident, you need to be clear about what you stand for professionally and in life. Write a 30–50 word statement such as one beginning, 'I am a highly-motivated and dedicated child-centred professional with a wide range of experience of . . .' Learn this statement off by heart and repeat it to yourself before you go into challenging meetings or situations.
- Try using affirmation statements such as:
  - o I choose to be hopeful and find optimistic ways to look at this.
  - o I might not be able to see the good in this situation at the moment, but it is there.
  - o I find hope and courage from deep inside me.
  - o I trust myself.
  - o I am not going to give up because I have not tried all possible options.
  - o I forgive myself for the mistakes that I make.
- Visualise success. Successful sportsmen and sportswomen visualise a successful outcome before an event, for example, the rugby player Johnny Wilkinson, would rehearse in his mind the ball going between the posts before taking a penalty kick. Try visualising successful outcomes to meetings or events. What does it look like? What does it feel like?
- List your achievements and remind yourself of them regularly. Keep your list somewhere private but where you will frequently see it, such as in the inside cover of a diary.
- Keep a folder of positive feedback, e.g. thank you cards, emails and newspaper clippings.

- List the things that you are grateful for. It can be a very positive and rewarding activity that will help to improve your self-image.
- Keep yourself well-groomed and dress well. Get your hair done and buy a new dress or suit. We tend to feel more confident when we are looking our best.
- Think about your posture. Standing tall or sitting straight projects confidence to other people. Avoid folding your arms as it looks defensive. Keep your hands still.
- Maintain eye contact and smile where appropriate.
- Speak slowly. Talking quickly can appear quite apologetic, as if you believe your views do not warrant the time for proper consideration.
- Use positive language, e.g. 'I believe' rather than 'I think'; 'I will' rather than 'I will try to'.
- Prepare. It would be difficult to go into any exam and feel confident about it without having prepared first. Good preparation, for any situation, can only help to boost our confidence levels.
- We cannot be experts in everything and will inevitably feel less confident in some areas. Explore ways to increase your competence levels in those areas.
- Set yourself small goals that contribute to larger projects, so that you experience success often.
- Find allies and mentors both within and outside the school gates.
- Comfort zones only shrink if we constantly stay within them, thus diminishing our confidence levels. Do something each week that takes you out of your comfort zone and you will find that your 'bubble' expands, increasing your confidence levels in the process.

Leadership interview

Wendy Rose – Headteacher, St. John's C of E Primary School, Ripley, Derbyshire

Background

St. John's is a large primary school with a nursery unit. It currently has 394 pupils on roll and serves a former mining town in mid Derbyshire. Wendy was my Co-Head in 2007/8. This is Wendy's second 'solo' headship.

Stressors

One of the most significant stressors for Wendy is the constant raising of expectations at a national level.

> *'The development state of your school is a significant factor in the level of stress you feel. If you have been judged in inspection to be 'good' or 'outstanding' you have, of course, the pressure of maintaining that grading, but you do have the affirmation that the system has already judged your school to be at least 'good'. I feel it would be easier to maintain a good or outstanding judgement than it is to attain it in the first place. It feels, at times, as though you can never actually achieve a target before the bar is raised again.'*

> *'With so many changes in policy and expectations in recent times, it is a constant pressure to keep up, particularly if the information is not being disseminated effectively. You are always worried that you might have missed something that might then have consequences in terms of Ofsted and HMI.'*

However, despite these pressures, it is child protection/safeguarding issues that cause Wendy the most stress.

> *'I find it very hard to stop thinking about the children in such cases and what is happening to them outside of school and that impacts on your own well-being. Apart from the emotional toll it takes on you, it is the amount of time you spend dealing with these situations and that takes you away from other tasks that you should be doing, creating further pressure.'*

Coping strategies

'I need to have the right systems in place to do the things that need to be done. I try to be very organised and keep on top of the workload. I would much rather stay late and complete a task than go home and be stressing all evening about not being on top of things. I don't have specific strategies or techniques for unwinding, though I do find a good workout is a great source of release! I love my job and my school and if I feel on top of things, I don't generally get stressed. (This seems a bit blasé of me!! I do get stressed, but not sure how you could change it!)'

The school was recently awarded the Inclusion Quality Mark and assessors identified the high levels of trust between people as being a real strength of the school.

'Having the confidence and professional trust in one another makes a huge difference to everybody when working under pressure.'

Wendy also feels, as a committed Christian, that the power of prayer has been a significant factor in her resilience over time.

Managing stress in others
Wendy believes that feeling appreciated can go a long way in helping staff manage their own stress levels.

'Giving people time towards completing tasks and not expecting people to complete everything in their own time is really important and is always appreciated.'

'Saying thank you is a small thing but makes a huge difference to people. Little things really do help people to feel valued. Buying biscuits for staff meetings or buying doughnuts always goes down well.'

'Having fun at work is important too. We try to have one staff meeting every half term that is not focused on raising standards, but has activities that promote team building and laughter.'

'We all also need someone that we can turn to at work and say, "I am not coping well today, I need some space" without fear of being judged. Not everyone will come to me, I know, but the important thing is that they have someone.'

If someone has a personal problem that is impacting on work, they will generally come to me and I will try to talk through what they have done already and what I might be able to do to support them. Giving people quality time to listen to them helps them to feel valued and that you care about them. Sometimes that might mean offering to take some responsibility away from them in the short term. Or offering: "Would it help if I give you a little more time to do this?" or, "Would it help if you missed. . .?"

If it is a work-related issue, I would put in some negotiated support, but the individual would have to accept that there is an issue first. I wouldn't take away the expectation of planning and marking – as these are fundamental expectations of the job.'

Advice to new headteachers or other senior leaders

'Teaching is not an easy job to pace yourself at – things need doing when they need doing. One of the keys to building resilience is teamwork. Knowing that you are in it together makes a real difference – support one another and learn from one another too.'

Summary: Chapter 7

- An Ofsted inspection is one of the top causes of stress because:

  1 it is the ultimate uncontrollable

  2 the goalposts are constantly shifting, creating uncertainty

  3 the stakes are getting higher and higher

  4 it is the one event that causes all school staff to be stressed simultaneously though not always for the same reasons.

- Understanding the key stressors for different groups of people can help us to manage both our own stress as well as that of the people we lead.

- The best preparation for inspection is to make a focus on teaching and learning your priority on a daily basis.

- Control all that you can.

  o Know and understand the framework and the criteria you are being judged against.

  o Know your data thoroughly.

o Have a plan in place of exactly what is going to happen when you receive the call.

o Have a plan of what you want inspectors to see.

o Have plans in place to respond to any 'known unknowns'.

- Take the mystery out of the process for staff by making sure that they are as well briefed as possible.

- Panic spreads. Staff need to see that you appear to be calm and in control – even if you are not feeling it.

- The pace of inspection is frenetic and exhausting. You need to be at your physical and mental best throughout. Don't ignore your own needs.

- Stay focused.

o Don't allow yourself to be distracted by decisions that seem unjust whilst the process is ongoing.

o Make sure you have a trusted colleague that you can ring and vent to during the inspection.

- Be true to yourself, what you believe in and what your school stands for.

8 'Habitudes' – Breaking patterns of thinking

No beating yourself up. That's not allowed. Be patient with yourself. It took you years to form the bad habits of thought that you no longer want. It will take a little time to form new and better ones.

Holly Mosier

I think that people who know me well would tell you that I have always been a bit of a worrier (all right, a lot of a worrier!) and that worry (often caused by an over concern about what other people think about me), intensified as I got older. It is hard to say whether that was actually a feature of ageing, or whether it was more to do with the increased responsibilities that successive promotions had brought with them. Either way, it had brought me to a position in 2006/7 where I could no longer function. My thinking habits and attitudes had become so ingrained that at first there seemed no way back.

For example, I was worried that I would stammer in meetings and so I did – a self-fulfilling prophecy.

'Repeated ingrained behaviours, or **habits,** *are generally accepted as the way in which your personality is demonstrated, so behaviours are often worth changing if they are unhelpful!'*

(Steve Peters, *The Chimp Paradox*, 2012)

I recently heard the author, Andy Cope, compare the way we think to across a grassy field. The first time we do it, our footsteps leave little impression. Repeat the same route several times and the grass becomes flattened, leaving a clear trail across the field. Repeat the same route enough times and the grass wears away all together leaving a very clear path that we will return to time and again.

We all knew that there would be significant hurdles to be overcome if I was to return to work, and both Chris and my GP knew that the timing of a planned return was essential *and* that I had first got to want to go back to work. After three months of absence, I was clear in my own mind that I did want to return. There was, admittedly, a financial element to the decision. However, despite what had happened to me, I loved my school and the community it served. It was not so much that I was afraid of returning to school itself, but I was anxious about going backwards and feeling those feelings of panic and being out of control, combined with the physical manifestations of stress that I had been experiencing.

It was clear to all concerned that any return to work was going to have to be gradual.

Most readers will be familiar with the notion of a phased return to work often starting with half days and building up in an agreed, negotiated manner until the employee is eventually able to return to full-time working. This process is kept under weekly review and the time-scale for a full return is often around four to six weeks. For someone returning after a physical illness or operation, this allows them time to get themselves back up to speed with what has been happening during their absence, whilst not over-tiring them as they recuperate. For people suffering from work-related anxiety or depression there is however, another facet to this process – *exposure*.

Graduated exposure to fears is a common approach to the treatment of phobias.

'Fears are common, but they become a problem – a phobia – when they are inappropriately intense and/or impair one's quality of life.'

(Helen Kennerley, *Overcoming Anxiety: A Self-help Guide to Using Cognitive Behavioural Techniques*)

Treatment of phobias needs to be graded and prolonged. It needs to be repeated and often practised (rather like homework). Thus, the treatment of someone suffering from arachnophobia (fear of spiders) might begin with a few seconds exposure to a toy spider. This would eventually lead to a real spider being in the room. Over the course of treatment, the length of exposure would increase and homework may include visualisation exercises such as imagining yourself in a room with a spider and remaining calm. The final outcome, unimaginable at the outset, would be to be able to hold a spider without feeling panic.

The aim of treatment is to build tolerance to the source of fear and desensitise our unwanted mental and physical response.

Chris says that the television programme, *I'm a Celebrity, Get Me Out of Here*, is a classic example of graduated exposure. Abandoned in the Australian outback, the ten or so celebrities spend most of the first night awake, fearful of whatever their strongest phobia might be, e.g. rats, snakes or insects. During the course of the ensuing 'bush tucker trials' they are exposed to more and more of their worst fears. For the handful of contestants that make it through to the third and final week without being voted off, they become increasingly desensitised to their fears and find themselves successfully dealing with phobias and situations that they could never have imagined being able to endure at the start of the process.

Aspects of the way that I had been feeling had elements of agoraphobia within them.

'Agoraphobia is not simply a fear of open spaces; it is the fear of leaving a place of safety, such as the home or a car or the doctor's surgery, or a combination of safe places.'
(Dr Helen Kennerley, *Overcoming Anxiety: A Self-help Guide to Using Cognitive Behavioural Techniques*)

Over the months, Chris had helped me to overcome a fear of leaving the house through gradual exposure to situations, such as walking the dog, shopping and going to the cinema.

My phased return to work in the Summer of 2007, allowed me the opportunity to gradually increase my exposure to the situation I had become fearful of. It was largely successful, due to the support of our Deputy and Assistant Heads who continued to be in charge of the school on a day by day basis. Having the support of my Assistant Head as co-Head for two terms played a big part in my successful return, along with the non-judgemental support of the governing body.

When I say it was largely successful, what I mean is that having built my hours back up during the phased return and starting to feel more comfortable, school broke up for the six week summer break. This period of time allowed me time to ruminate and whilst my anxiety levels certainly did not return to anywhere near the levels they had been at, they did increase over the six weeks.

Chris says it is one of the reasons why school holidays have a negative impact on the treatment of children who have school phobia. You can spend months trying to desensitise them to the school environment only to find that the six week break puts things back to square one.

Challenge

Whilst many people suffering from phobias need professional support, there are some lower issues we can reflect upon ourselves.

What things in life (not necessarily at work) cause you to worry excessively and bring about inappropriately-intense reactions?

What might a graduated plan of exposure look like for you?

Much of my thinking had become ingrained and with familiar triggers bringing predictable responses.

Here are two issues that Chris helped me to address:

Issue 1

As discussed in chapter 1 (page 10), I would often have panic attacks on the way to work. These usually occurred at the same roundabout and I would often end up pulling over in a nearby layby getting myself into a dreadful state. (Interestingly, passing the same roundabout on the way back home was never an issue!)

Chris's solution: 'Don't use *that* A road to get to work and don't pass that roundabout where you have grown to expect a panic attack.'

I stopped travelling on that route, even though it was the most direct one. Instead, I devised four other different routes that I would vary on impulse. I stopped treading the same worn path across the grassy field and started to invent others that I travelled less frequently and actually found I enjoyed the variety of the slightly longer but more picturesque routes. It felt less predictable and less like I was getting on the same old rollercoaster each morning.

I never had a panic attack on the way to work after that.

Issue 2

Now, you are going to have to bear with me a little with this second one as it is not particularly pleasant! In fact, if you are of a squeamish disposition you might want to skip the next two or three paragraphs altogether!

I was often very nauseous in the mornings before work. I would get up each morning, get dressed, and eat exactly the same type of cereal as the day before. I would then take the dog out for a walk, where I would start to ruminate on what *might* happen during the day ahead.

Having got back, I would go to the bathroom to clean my teeth and then I would often 'revisit my breakfast'. It became routine behaviour over time, eventually leading me to think that there was actually no point in having breakfast in the first place – it was a waste of cereal! Of course, not having anything inside you is hardly the best set-up for coping with the day ahead, but I truly saw no point to it. However, even with no food inside me the act of cleaning my teeth was now part of this horribly familiar routine and I came to associate cleaning my teeth with retching. (Although again, interestingly not at night). I was anxious about it happening and so predictably it did – a vicious circle and a self-fulfilling prophecy neatly rolled into one bundle of misery.

Chris's solution: Well, you may well have guessed that he would have emphasised the importance of eating something in the morning in order to have a release of energy during the day. You may too have guessed that he suggested that I varied what I had to eat, so that the whole breakfast experience was not just 'Groundhog Day'. But, what about cleaning my teeth? Clearly not cleaning them would have been one option, if somewhat unpleasant. Chris believed that the nausea was all about anticipation of what might happen, but stressed that anticipation was usually worse than the reality. (He was right in fairness – few days were ever as bad as I had built them up to be.) Chris suggested I kept a tube of toothpaste and a toothbrush in my office and then cleaned my teeth once I had settled into being in the environment and my anxiety levels had subsided. No one was likely to know and what did it actually matter if they did?

It worked.

In both instances what Chris suggested were not major changes in lifestyle or behaviour but simple, small changes to a routine that were sufficient to break an ingrained pattern of thinking and behaviour and set me off in new directions across that grassy field. Looking back, the answers to those two problems are almost absurdly obvious, but at the time I simply could not see the wood for the trees.

Challenge

What patterns of behaviour do you recognise in yourself that are unhelpful to you but have become ingrained?

What small changes to your routines could you make that could disrupt the vicious circle of thoughts and behaviour?

Most people who know me well will tell you that over the years I have had a tendency to catastrophise.

Catastrophisation is the ability to exaggerate the significance of negative events and project and assume the worst possible consequences from them.

I would like to think that I *do* have some fine characteristics in my personality, but the ability to catastrophise is certainly not one of them. On the plus side, if you have a tendency towards catastrophisation, you will never ever be bored because even on a day when things are going well, and you should not need to feel stress at all, you will anticipate negative outcomes to a sequence of events that may not have even happened yet. On the downside, you waste endless energy worrying about things that may not come to pass.

'A day of worry is more exhausting than a week of work.'

(Sir John Lubbock)

I have previously talked about the fact I could waste whole days worrying about a parent who has booked an appointment for an unknown reason. Often they were not complaints at all, and even if they were, I usually had the experience and skill sets to be able to resolve the issue, but that would not stop me ruminating. Sometimes there was justification for my anxieties and concerns, but at other times I made mountains out of molehills and failed to take my Grandma's consistent advice when I was young: 'Let's cross that bridge when we get there'.

In all honesty, I don't think I will ever completely 'park' that aspect of my personality, but I am getting much better at it.

One of the best strategies I have found for countering the tendency to catastrophise, is to have my thinking challenged.

Talking to other people and not bottling things up is really important as you will hear a number of the leaders who are interviewed in this book state clearly. Talking and sharing our concerns with a trusted supporter inside, or outside, the workplace allows us the opportunity to have our worst-case scenarios and worrisome thoughts positively challenged.

Don't be afraid to say to people, 'This is what I am worrying about. Is there another way of looking at this situation?' Most people are only too glad to be asked.

It is also good to develop the skill of challenging your own thinking. Many fears are irrational and ill-formed thoughts. Getting things down on paper often helps provide us with some clarity. For example, for many people, writing a 'to do list' helps them to order their thoughts and prioritise their actions. Equally, writing down our fears can be an important step to gaining perspective.

Helen Kennerley suggests five questions that we can usefully apply to challenge our own thinking:

*'1. Are there any reasons **for** my having this worrying thought?'*

What have I experienced, seen or read, that has caused me to have this worry? There is usually a root cause so we should not feel embarrassed about it.

I knew a teacher who catastrophised about lesson observations after she had had one disastrous one. There was a clear root cause to her anxiety.

*'2. Are there any reasons **against** me holding this thought?'*

If someone was going to argue why my fear was not rational, what is it they would say?

The same teacher had been observed on a number of occasions before and since and had always received good feedback.

'3. What is the worst thing that could happen?'

Uncomfortable though it is, imagining the worst-case scenario can actually help us deal with it.

Should she have had another difficult lesson, the situation was not life-threatening. Nor would it mean losing her job. The worst-case scenario was likely to be that she would be re-observed and offered support.

'4. How would I cope with this?'

Knowing the worst-case scenario allows us to plan for it and planning gives us some much needed mental control over the situation.

She might ask to talk to someone else outside the situation or ask for the opportunity to observe good practice elsewhere, for example.

'5. What is a more constructive way of looking at this situation?'

She has only had one unsatisfactory observation out of several! Her pupil progress results are good! This could be a good opportunity to reinvigorate her practice by observing someone for whom this subject area is a real strength.

Having gone through these questions, it is helpful to write yourself a short paragraph in conclusion that summarises the main points of your responses. This helps to provide some insight into the appropriateness of the anxiety you are feeling.

This is a really helpful technique but takes some time, and as with most things, some practice.

Chris taught me another shorter technique that covers some of the same points.

A sense of perspective

I would divide an A4 piece of paper in half. In the left-hand column I would write down things that I was worried or anxious about and score them on a scale of 1 to 10, with 1 being mildly worrying (but not enough to keep me awake at night) through to 10 life-threatening. The scale would take in sleepless nights and potentially career ending along the way! I found that attaching a value to my worries enabled me to keep some perspective and also mentally prioritise what I needed to worry about. Next to the issue, in the right-hand column I would make myself write down a positive response. So for example, if the area of worry was that there was a dip in results in one year group, I would write that results in almost all year groups remain good. Alternatively, if there had been a fight on the playground that was going to be difficult to address with parents, I would remind myself in the right-hand column that thankfully, nobody was seriously hurt.

Challenge

You may want to try mapping some of the issues that are causing you worry or anxiety onto the grid below, or create one of your own.

What is my worry or anxiety?	Where is the issue on a scale of 1 to 10 ?	What is an alternative way of looking at the situation?

When I had to challenge my own thinking, I had to remind myself of three other things that sometimes clouded my judgement and thinking which Chris said that I had a tendency to do. I remember these as: BEG.

BEG

Black and white thinking: I would tend to see things in absolutes, all or nothing, win or lose, succeed or fail. When calm I know that many issues are shades of grey.

Exaggerate: I would often exaggerate situations or things that had been said, making them more of an issue to deal with than they needed to be.

Genaralise: because of one bad experience in a situation, I would mentally project the stress of that situation on to other similar but unrelated situations.

So when we are worried or fearful, we need to ask ourselves honestly if we are also bringing unhelpful **BEG** behaviour to the issue.

When stressed, being told that you need to 'snap out of it' is the last thing you need to hear. If you knew how to 'snap out of it' you would!

Distraction is often the key to ruminating on issues.

Allen Elkin PhD, advocates the use of 'stop' techniques such as this one.

Stop technique

'Simply take an ordinary rubber band and put it around your wrist. Now, whenever you notice an intrusive or unwanted thought crowding your thinking, pull the elastic and let it snap to your wrist. This shouldn't be painful – just a sharp reminder that you want this distressing thought to go.'

(Allen Elkin, 2013)

Dr Rick Norris wrote a wonderful book, *The Promised Land*, (2006) which I read whilst I was away from work. In it, he draws upon his many years of counselling to highlight the link between stress, anxiety and depression. He compares the mind to a DVD library.

The mind as a DVD library

'When we are depressed, we subconsciously start to do things. Firstly we play the predominantly negative DVD memories from the past. Secondly we find it increasingly difficult to focus on the positive aspects of any of our DVD memories.'

(Rick Norris, *The Promised Land: A Guide to Positive Thinking for Sufferers of Stress, Anxiety and Depression,* 2006)

Rick also goes on to talk about the curse of self-doubt.

'The negative DVD memories contain images of ourselves in the situations where we are struggling to cope and this causes us to doubt our ability to handle the situation successfully. In turn this starts to impact on our self-esteem.'

(Rick Norris, *The Promised Land: A Guide to Positive Thinking for Sufferers of Stress, Anxiety and Depression,* 2006)

Rick advocates that we create a DVD library of our top ten happy DVD memories, e.g. a wedding, or a holiday with family or friends etc. We then draw upon this library when we are feeling stressed or distressed.

I often used to find that I would recycle negative memories, particularly difficult meetings or conversations, as I lay in bed at night. I would replay the image as a film over and over again.

Chris taught me to:

1 Freeze the image of the memory that was disturbing me so that it became a still, rather than a moving image.
2 Gradually drain the colour from the image, so that it became black and white.
3 Imagine the image shrinking in size, simultaneously reducing to a dot on the horizon.
4 Pick a happy memory (from your top ten DVD list).
5 Bring the still image (the cover of the DVD) forward from a dot on the horizon so that it gets larger and fills the 'full screen'.

6 Enhance the colours of the image so that they become bright and vivid.

7 Run the image as a movie, recalling the full sensory experience of how you felt, what you saw, heard and smelt.

I found this technique really helpful in banishing unwelcome thoughts.

Challenge

What are your top ten happiest memories that you would place in your DVD library?

1

2

3

4

5

6

7

8

9

10

Try running one of these every day for the next ten days.

Many of the people who I have interviewed for this book have managed to stay resilient, in part because they are able to relax and distract themselves from the things that cause them stress. They do this in a wide variety of ways from running, to songwriting, to watching films, learning a foreign language, travelling or spending time with family and friends. It is so important to have that distraction, to keep your mind occupied in other ways and avoid the spiralling trap of rumination.

During 2014, I surveyed 100 school leaders about their favourite activities for distraction and relaxation and although this has a slightly worryingly *Family Fortunes* feel to it, I think it is worth sharing the top ten most popular in the hope that it might inspire you! In the hope that a producer from BBC2, Channel 4 or Channel 5 is reading this and feels inspired to make one of those three hour 'Greatest Moments'-style programmes, I will count down from ten to one (TV executives – I actually have the numbers from 50!)

10th – Maintaining a hobby
9th – Planning regular treats, such as going away
8th – Food – cooking/eating out
7th – Listening to music
6th – Off-loading to friends/socialising
5th – Watching TV/films/theatre
4th – Reading
3rd – Drinking a glass of wine or beer
2nd – Time spent with family
1st – Walking (with or without a dog!)

Take control . . .

Emotion regulation

Our emotions are sometimes compared to the waves of the sea: sometimes the sea is flat, calm and welcoming; at other times it can be very rough with high crashing waves. The sea is very changeable and so are human emotions. Sometimes we can see a storm coming; sometimes it appears out of nowhere and threatens to engulf us. Emotional regulation is about learning to ride the waves, recognise the signs of how we are feeling and adapt our behaviour to ensure that we are not swept away, whilst ensuring our behaviour is socially acceptable.

- Emotions often help us to act quickly or instinctively. Our fear, for example, can keep us from harm.
- Negative feelings are not always a bad thing.
- Our mind can take extreme emotions and incorrectly convert them to facts or beliefs about ourselves. For example, 'If I am afraid of something the worst will inevitably happen.' Or, 'I feel inadequate at my job therefore I must be inadequate.' Thoughts do not equate to facts.
- Your emotions have validity. There is no correct way to feel in every situation we experience.
- Take responsibility for your emotions rather than blaming them on others. Taking ownership is an important step in being able to manage them.
- We need to recognise when our emotions are becoming destructive and ask for help. Letting others know when we are feeling bad is not a weakness.
- Know what your emotional triggers are and why you respond in the way that you do. Is there an alternative way of looking at the situation?
- Have a plan. Having identified unhelpful emotions, know what strategies you are going to use to help deal with the situation, e.g. go for coffee with a trusted friend to talk about your feelings.
- Write a list of things that you either currently enjoy or used to enjoy doing, however small, and do one of these a day, e.g. run a hot bath.

- Keep a list of the positive things that have happened during the day.
- Avoid breaking up positive experiences by worrying about what will happen when they end. So, for example, make the most of your holiday and enjoy the positives about the experience, rather than focussing on your return to work.
- When you feel your mind drifting towards the negative, refocus, e.g. do a crossword or listen to an audio book to keep your mind occupied.
- Try to do at least one thing a day that makes you feel in control of your life.
- Break down big goals that seem overwhelming into very small steps. Try to take a step a day so that you feel that you are making progress.
- We all make mistakes. Apologise where appropriate, rectify or limit the damage where you can and then move on and let it go. Don't beat yourself up about it.
- Tackle your fears, don't avoid them – otherwise they will continue to grow. Overcoming a fear gives you confidence, self-respect and makes you feel in control.
- Try prayer or meditation.
- Make sure that you look after your body. Treat physical illnesses, take regular exercise, avoid drinking alcohol as a crutch, eat a balanced diet and try to maintain a regular sleep pattern.

Leadership interview

David Bateson OBE – Education Consultant and former Executive Principal, Ash Field Academy, Leicester and former Headteacher, Dawn House School, Rainworth, Nottinghamshire

Background

Until 2014, David was Executive Principal of a day and residential national teaching school for learners of all abilities and disabilities aged 4–19 from across several LEAs. There were 125 pupils on roll. The main presenting difficulty of pupils is physical, often allied to one or more additional needs of a communication, medical, learning, sensory or progressive nature. Approximately a quarter of pupils have no oral communication and a quarter have progressive conditions. All of them have an unquenchable desire for life and an indomitable spirit. The range of achievement in the school might best be indicated by comparing students in the FE department: some have several GCSEs; others might developmentally be pre-school.

The school has held a number of specialist status designations. It is currently a national teaching school focusing on underachievement and special educational needs and disability.

Ofsted has judged the school as 'outstanding' eleven times: five times in day inspections and six times in stand-alone residential inspections. In 2014, the school supported another school to come out of 'Requires Improvement' where David acted as a temporary executive head.

Since 1995 David has combined headship with, amongst other things, being a national leader in education, a primary Ofsted inspector, an external adviser in secondary schools, and a trustee of eight education charities, including a national teaching school.

He has worked on a number of bodies, including the DfE and the Cabinet Office working parties. He is a local and national leader of education and currently chairs the National Special Educational Needs Forum.

Stressors

David stated from the outset that all these comments are entirely personal and that he is not attempting to represent anyone else. He said it is a foolish head that thinks they are immune to a catastrophic reaction to the pressures of the role and recognises that in his career he has experienced two, thankfully short, episodes where he was unable to speak and drive for a time. He also experienced periods of being under medication to help him sleep, having been an insomniac for 30 years. On one occasion, he put on his best suit at midnight before an Ofsted inspection and waited for them to arrive. As he observes, he felt that for him:

'There are two terrible places to be: special measures and the fear of losing the status of "outstanding". Both are precipitated.'

'The truth is that many factors can act as stressors, differentially, over a period of time. We all need optimal stress and I'm no martyr to the job: I love it and nobody made me do it. The job is, and should be, stressful given that it is high profile, important and rightly accountable. Inspections and fighting to keep our school open in a context where special schools could be seen as not just unnecessary but, in some university and political circles, evil, were always the macro stressors.

Trying, in our context, to meet the challenge of meeting the full curriculum from Foundation Stage to Further Education can be a pressure just as, in a different way, if one was in a school where there are difficulties with a governor it can be. Fortunately, the governors were very supportive.

The biggest emotional stressor was always the loss of a child. Nothing prepares one for that. At a practical level, a big stressor can be managing the budget. Special needs pupils attract higher levels of funding and the volatility of funding is difficult to plan for: the loss of a pupil, either through movement or, tragically, through bereavement can have a massive and highly unpredictable impact, not only on the school community but also on the school's budget and on people's jobs.'

'As the school has a residential element to it, days can be very long and as head, you are still responsible for what happens in the other sixteen hours outside the normal school day.'

'Parents have been a great source of support and shown remarkable good humour and fortitude in doing the best for their children. This aided our work considerably. Very rarely and inadvertently, parents and our own actions or inactions could, however, be a source of stress for wholly understandable reasons.'

'Sometimes we simply got it wrong, for example with a miscommunication, and then honesty is the best policy. With the medical and care side being such a priority, parents would obviously be concerned. Sometimes I found it hard to communicate well over differences in perception of the achievement of a child. Naturally, as head, one is the available and natural conduit for concerns and it is stressful to not be able to satisfy expectation.'

Some pupils at the school have progressive conditions which means that they may not reach adulthood. The passing of any pupil would always bring back those lost before.

'It does something to you and so it should'.

David would often be asked to give the eulogy.

'Giving a eulogy is both a great honour and a great weight. You have only one chance to get it right and you want to avoid platitudes. You want to respect and dignify the child and family without sentimentalising.

Every day at school needs to be the very best it can be because one of their days may well be worth three or four of yours.'

Coping strategies

David describes himself as an adrenaline junkie but says that for him the true stress comes in dealing with repetitive issues, for example, staffing matters. It was important to him to keep reinventing the school, aiming to be an outward-looking centre of expertise – it kept the school improving and renewing.

'When I look at what many of our students are having to deal with, I do remind myself, "What right do I have to feel bad?"'

David lives some distance from the school which means, much as he likes them, there is little chance of bumping into people connected with work. He sees it as important to have another life and that way you bring more to your work. When at home he throws himself into music, writing songs, playing in bands and recording albums.

'My guitar is like other people's cigarettes. I also enjoy a glass of wine and am lucky to have a supportive wife.'

Having highly-developed routines and expectations provides the basis for people to thrive. It protects them on an off day.

> 'Realise that optimum stress is vital to doing a good job. No one is immune from experiencing stress at times, but we can develop coping strategies even if that means recognising that you need a change.'

David believes that, whilst most leaders try to protect their staff from some of the pressures cascading down from above them, overprotecting people does them few favours in the long run.

> 'One of the best ways of preventing stress in staff is by spreading your belief in them, "You can do this!"
>
> Show them that you value them – it is so important that staff feel both valued and trusted. Ensure accountability, but make sure you have mechanisms in place to support people to be their best.'

> 'Make sure that people realise that you can make mistakes and that you will be supported. You need to judge the behaviour and not the person.'

> 'Themed dressing-up days – where people are allowed to be a little bonkers whilst maintaining professionalism – are important in school. We also subscribe to a helpline for staff too.'

Advice to new headteachers or other senior leaders

> 'You need to reconcile yourself to the fact that it is an impossible job. You will never know enough or have enough resources – don't beat yourself up about it.'

> 'Appoint supportive but challenging people to the staff, especially the senior team, and to the governing body.'

> 'Always have time for people, to have a joke and stay upbeat.'

> 'You need a sheer expectation that things will run like clockwork. I never chase deadlines – people like to know where they stand and what is coming up next. The better the systems and structures you have in place, the easier this is to achieve. Being organised is what gives you the space to be creative.'

> 'The job is a marathon not a sprint, but a marathon is much more enjoyable if the scenery changes. Don't be afraid to reinvent your school or take on some small-scale research and development.'

> 'Give your staff the same opportunities for variety too, through secondments, sabbaticals, internships and role swaps, e.g. Key Stage 1 to Key Stage 2 Team Leader. Build variety into your Performance Management Structure.'

> 'Refresh and renew.'

Summary: Chapter 8

- The more we revisit thoughts and behaviours, the more ingrained they become.
- Graduated exposure to our fears helps us to become desensitised to them.
- Exposure to our fears needs to be gradual, prolonged, repeated and practised in order to be effective.
- Small changes in routines and habits can go a long way to disrupting ingrained patterns of negative thinking and consequential behaviours.
- Catastrophisation is the exaggeration of the significance of negative events and the assumption of the worst possible outcomes of those events.
- We need to challenge the basis and rationality of our fears in order to successfully deal with them.
- Distraction techniques help to keep us from dwelling on our worries.

9 Staying positive – Keeping your head above water

Pearls don't lie on the seashore. If you want one, you must dive for it.

Chinese proverb

'Positive thinking in itself will not change the world, it has to be combined with decisions and action. However, in itself it is a massive start and it has been proven that positive thoughts actually enhance our health – not surprising really, given that stressful ones clearly do not help us.'

(David Taylor, *The Naked Leader*, 2002)

Jeremy Sutcliffe, in his book *8 Qualities of Successful School Leaders: The Desert Island Challenge*, (2013) asks some of the UK's most successful headteachers the following question:

'Imagine you were cast adrift on a desert island with a school full of children in desperate need of a great headteacher. What 8 qualities would you take with you to run your desert island school?'

(Jeremy Sutcliffe, 2013)

High up the list of qualities most commonly identified by the heads is *optimism*.

All the educational leaders that I have met and interviewed in the course of this book have combined passion for the job with a strong sense of moral purpose and optimism.

It seems to me that optimism and positivity go hand in hand, and that it is difficult to have one without the other. The truly great leaders are, I believe, not only able to maintain that sense of positivity and optimism in themselves but also inspire those qualities in the people they lead.

I realised as I returned to work after my illness, that it would be very difficult for me to be optimistic for the future if I could not feel more positive about the present. Moreover, how could I expect other people to be positive and optimistic if I could not manage it myself? I realised I needed to change my outlook.

'Happiness is an attitude. We either make ourselves miserable, or happy and strong. The amount of work is the same.'

(Francesca Reigler)

Realising that I needed to change was the first step on a journey (I cringe at using that cliché – I feel like a contestant on *The X Factor*, but I don't know how else I can put it). There have been setbacks along the way but I remain on an upward trajectory.

There are a number of strategies that I have learnt, and concepts that I have encountered that have helped me to recalibrate my thinking and behaviour and adopt a more positive outlook on life.

Firstly, I have come to realise that we all have mental filters. Our brains, highly sophisticated though they are, cannot deal with all the information that our senses bombard them with and so they filter out information that seems irrelevant.

It is true, that we only see what it is we are looking for.

I now work across the UK as a speaker and trainer and as such, I am running up many more miles per year on my car than I did when I was a headteacher and making the same shuttle run each day. My Ford Mondeo estate has served me well, but it is approaching 80,000 miles and things are starting to go wrong and it needs replacing. (If you are a reader of AutoTrader however it is mint condition and very reasonably priced!) The kids have all finished university now and so in many ways I don't need a big estate for those joyous start and end of term pickups where you feel like you are driving a removal van. However, I have a very large golden retriever, Eddie, who goes everywhere with me and he needs a big boot. Essentially, I want a car that is smaller on the outside but as big on the inside which is a tall order – I really need a Tardis!

I spoke to my son, Jonathan, who works in the business side of a fleet car sales company, and asked him what my options might be. He asked if I had considered a Hyundai i40, as they were good value for money, had a high spec and would be economical to run. I had to say, in all honesty that I had not considered a Hyundai i40, not because I was against the idea but because I had never even heard of it yet alone seen one. I went on the internet and found images of the car. I now not only know what they look like, but I see them frequently when I am out driving. They are everywhere – I am even considering buying one!

They are not new cars – they have been around for a while. I have just not noticed them before.

What we see largely depends on what our minds are looking for.

I had become so focussed at work on worrying about things that might never happen, that my brain had been filtering out the positives that were going on around me.

I made a real 'rookie' mistake early on in my first headship. I threw away a letter of complaint from a parent some six months after I had successfully (or so I thought) resolved the issue. Of course the issue reared its ugly head again about a year later and the parent referenced me to what they had said in their previous correspondence, which obviously I no longer had. Never having been blessed with the best of memories, I could not recall the details of the original incident, which despite my acting abilities clearly showed in the ensuing meeting with parents. It was not my finest hour.

From that point on, I archived any complaint in a red folder on the bookcase in my office. Whilst we really did not get that many, both of my headships were in big schools and inevitably over fifteen years the file became rather full. I tried to avoid the 'red file' but whenever I had to open it to clip in another letter or print off an email, I would find myself drawn like a moth to a flame and would paw over the contents. It was not the most edifying experience but then I recalled that Pam, who I had worked with for eight years, used to have a file in the filing cabinet in her office marked 'Treasures'. I set up a green file to sit next to the red one and I clipped into it a copy of an email that I had recently received from a member of the public complimenting the behaviour of our Year 1s when they had been out on a school visit the previous day. I added to it a collection of thank you cards from parents whose children were leaving for secondary school and a card from a pupil telling me I was the 'best headteacher in the world'. Over the coming months, I was able to clip many more things into the green file and on the occasions I did have to clip items into the red file, I would get the green one out and bury my head in that instead.

My friend, Peter, is one of the nicest guys you will meet. He likens this filtering out of the positives to a fault with your emails. All the positive emails are diverting to our junk folder instead of our inbox. As most of us don't often check our junk folder, we focus instead on the negative messages that are in our inbox.

I needed to reset my filters so that I was not 'spamming' the positives. Chris suggested that I kept a diary at work and before I left school each evening I should write down three good things that had happened each day. At first it was not always easy to examine the day retrospectively, but after a while I noticed that I was starting to be on the hunt for things, as they happened, knowing I needed to fill in the diary later. They were often small things like a child saying that they liked my tie, or a member of staff that said they had really enjoyed the story that I had told in assembly, but I would make sure I remembered them for when I filled in the diary. After a time, I started to look for positives and would end up having more than three things to write down at the end of the day! It also meant the last thing I would do at work was leave concentrating on the positive things that had happened during the day rather than the negative.

Secondly, whilst life is not always smooth-running and most of us suffer setbacks at some stage or another, I believe that some of the pressures that we experience are brought on by a dissatisfaction with what we have in life.

It seems at times that the whole purpose of advertising is to sow the seeds of dissatisfaction with what we currently have so that we will go out and buy whatever product they wish to sell us. Glossy lifestyle magazines bombard us with photographs and images of what our lives *ought* to be like. All these messages register with us on some level or another and if we are not careful, we can be sucked in. We can see our glass as half empty rather than half full.

Whilst I am not suggesting that we should lack ambition or satisfy ourselves with the status quo, I do believe that appreciating the things that we have got in life aids us in staying positive.

I once heard Peter issue the following challenge to delegates on a course.

Write a list of twenty things that you really do appreciate in life but often take for granted.

1

2

3

4

5

6

7

8

9

10

11

12

13

14

15

16

17

18

19

20

Peter then went on to challenge people to add to that list every day for the next fortnight.

It's a valuable exercise that can give our reserves of positivity a real boost. Regularly counting your blessings certainly does help you to see your glass as half full.

We really do see what we are looking for. If we are looking for the negatives, we will find them in abundance. If we are looking for the positives, well they are out there too, we just sometimes need to reset our filters in order to see them.

Thirdly, one of the reasons why I became overwhelmed by my role was that I frequently got to the end of a working day feeling I had achieved little and had made little impact on my to do list. There were a number of reasons for this, but one of them was certainly that I did not plan my time well enough.

Part of the reason for my frustration was that I would write down *anything* that needed doing on my to do list creating a lengthy document with unrealistic expectations of my own ability to action them.

I plan more nowadays and whilst I still have a 'master list' of things that need to be achieved, I also have daily lists which I divide into three columns:

Must do today	Should do today	Could do today

This has helped me to better prioritise what I need to do. But, even if you don't make it as far as the second column, you still finish the day with some satisfaction that you have hopefully actioned everything in your 'must do' column.

I always include some 'quick wins' on my list too. These are often small things that can be speedily achieved adding to a sense of accomplishment.

Whilst I did not always organise my time as well as I might have, my lack of impact on my to do lists was not because I was twiddling my thumbs. With 800 pupils and even with a non-teaching Deputy, there were plenty of unplanned events that could knock me off course from what I was setting out to achieve. Anything from sorting out a bullying issue to the fire alarm being set off by a water heater with a faulty thermostat, to the Police Community Support Officer wanting to discuss the parking outside the school, to an unfamiliar and estranged parent turning up unexpectedly demanding to see their child, or the local radio station ringing to ask for comments on a planning application for more housing in the school's catchment area. Issues such as these are of course part and parcel of leading a school. They are also what make the job varied and interesting. They do however, along with unexpected emails, letters and phone calls, take up significant periods of time that you haven't planned for.

I learnt to keep a 'Have done but didn't plan to' list and briefly logged all the unplanned activities I had engaged in during the day. On the days that I had not achieved what I had set out to achieve (and there were many of them), I would review the list of what I had actually achieved alongside it. I still do this and on the days when I have not accomplished everything I might have wanted, instead of beating myself up about it I try to remind myself of what I *have* achieved.

Feeling that you are achieving and making an impact is so important to staying positive and resilient. When decorating, I enjoy hanging wallpaper because I can visibly see what I am achieving. I dislike emulsioning walls, particularly if it is with the same colour, because I cannot see the impact I am having.

Another thing that has helped me greatly has been music. I have no great talent for it (the dizzy heights of my accomplishments being reaching the position of third bugler in the Boys' Brigade in 1977. I had been sixth at one stage – unfortunately it was not a reflection of me getting any better, more that other boys were getting older and leaving) – but listening to music transports me to different periods in time. I have a great talent for recognising eighties pop by the opening bars, or for being 'sad' as my children would put it.

Studies in music therapy have found that music can actually affect your physiology.

I find that listening to music evokes quite strong emotional responses. In the days of cassette tapes I would drive my wife mad by spending the day before going on holiday compiling mixed tapes to play to the kids in the car. So, it will come as no surprise to you that, despite being a bit of a luddite in many respects (e.g. I cannot use the tracker pad on my laptop, I have to use a mouse), I love iTunes! As well as recreating what must be the entire jukebox from my days in the Student Union bar, I create themed playlists. I have playlists of upbeat music such as *Beautiful Day* by U2, *Happy* by Pharrell Williams and *Mr Blue Sky* by Electric Light Orchestra. I have lists of calming classical music to unwind to and for when I am writing. I also have a playlist for when I need to dig deep and find courage, e.g. *Be Still* by The Killers, *Search for the Hero* by M People and *Proud* by Heather Small. I am embarrassed to report to you that the theme from *Rocky* also features in there too. I think my children, Jonathan, Charlotte and Julia are probably right. I *am* sad.

Listening to these ever-evolving playlists enables me to connect with the emotions I want to feel.

One factor behind my illness in 2006/2007 was that I had become incredibly isolated. This was no one's fault other than my own, but it left me ploughing my own furrow with my head down, rarely looking up to take in what was happening in the wider educational landscape. This had several effects.

- Firstly, it cut me off from a group of people (other headteachers) who could have been an important source of support and best placed to understand the pressures of the job.
- Secondly, it meant that I was not having my thinking challenged by exposure to new ideas, thus leading to a narrowing of thinking.
- Thirdly, I lost perspective by concentrating on my problems and issues without putting them into the context of what other people were dealing with.

I knew, returning to work, that I had to expand my comfort zone – my bubble of safety – which, when I was at my worst, was no larger than the confines of my house.

As I became more comfortable back at work, I joined a leadership network at the National College of School Leadership. One thing led to another and I was invited to join the Primary Reference Group, a group of heads providing advice and acting as a sounding board to Paul Bennett, The Director of Primary Leadership. This was a group of dynamic, forward-thinking heads with a variety of viewpoints on a whole range of issues and they were actually interested in what I thought and had to say. At first, I wasn't sure why anyone would want to listen to my opinions, but these meetings increased my confidence and expanded my thinking and I was grateful for the opportunity, and for the time spent with the other members of the group, whose wide variety of viewpoints challenged my own thinking and gave me back some of the broader perspective on education which I had lost. I found that my views were valued and that I did have something to say. Engaging with the Primary Reference Group led to work on a variety of advisory and project management groups within the college as well as input into the design of some programmes such as The Executive Head training provision.

The work would, on average, take me out of school a couple of times a month. But more importantly, it helped to rebuild my confidence and expand my comfort zone. It gave me a heads up on what was coming up on the national education agenda. It exposed me to new ideas and alternative viewpoints and most important of all, it gave me space and time to reflect, something that I had previously not been very good at.

Another thing that helped me, following on from reading Dr Rick Norris's book *The Promised Land*, was a growing acceptance that 'into every life a little rain must fall'. Things will go wrong. Some of these may be preventable and others not.

'You need to reconcile yourself to the fact that it is an impossible job. You will never know enough or have enough resources – don't beat yourself up about it.'

David Bateson

It was in 2010 that I first met Andy Cope. On recommendation, I had booked him to come and run a half-day training session with our staff, which was very well received. As well as being a best-selling children's author, Andy was studying for a PhD in positive psychology and happiness through Loughborough University and had written, with Andy Whittaker, *The Art of Being Brilliant* based on Andy C's research.

Andy's aim is to share some of the 'secrets' of positive psychology, focusing on learning new habits of thinking and behaviour that will sustain 'personal brilliance' with no jargon or fancy words! As well as boosting morale, three of Andy's messages on that day particularly resonated with me.

- Firstly: we have to take personal responsibility for ourselves – nobody is in charge of our happiness except us.
- Secondly: there is only about ten percent of 'stuff' in life over which we have no control. The other ninety percent is about how we choose to react. Realising that started to make me believe that I had more control in life than I had previously thought.
- Thirdly, and most importantly: whilst it is not rocket science, the choice to be positive is a personal one. We can choose whether to be positive or not.

These concepts were not a miracle cure and, as Andy himself would say, 'it takes practice'. But, do you know what? I am getting better at it!

I stayed in touch with Andy and since leaving headship to work as a speaker and to write this book, I have greatly enjoyed working with him for part of the time, delivering sessions on *The Art of Being Brilliant*, at conferences and universities, businesses and schools.

Being positive is not always easy. In fact, it can be really difficult at times, but I do believe it is a key strength that I have observed in many people who manage to stay resilient over time.

' If I have the belief that I can do it, I shall surely acquire the capacity to do it even if I may not have it at the beginning.'

Mahatma Gandhi

Take control . . .

Mindfulness

The use of the word 'mindfulness' is on the increase. Even though mindfulness meditation has been around for hundreds if not thousands of years, the practice of mindfulness has been steadily growing in popularity and is gaining credence with the medical and mental health community. We live in a world that is getting ever busier and more hectic. We often live life at a frantic pace, so focused on targets and deadlines that we often miss appreciating some basic sensory information that is being fed to our brains about what is going on in the here and now.

Studies have demonstrated that people who practise mindfulness regularly, experience positive changes in their sense of well-being, their ability to concentrate, and their capacity to enjoy life.

Mindfulness is a practice that originated in Buddhism, but you don't need to be a Buddhist or even religious to gain from it.

Give yourself some time and space to consider the following:

- Thoughts are simply thoughts; they are not facts and you don't need to believe them or react to them.
- Your mind likes to constantly judge. Don't take your mind or its judgements too seriously. Practise listening without making judgments. Listen to understand rather than feeling pressured to respond and act.
- Stop what you're doing or thinking when someone is speaking to you, and really listen to them and pay attention.
- At the start of your working day, take a couple of moments to breathe deeply and set yourself the intention to stay calm, present and focused throughout the day.
- Spend time in nature noticing the smells, the noise and the passing of the seasons.
- Try to eat slowly, really smelling and tasting the food whilst noticing its texture in your mouth. Eat at least once a week without the distraction of the television or the radio in the background.
- Take time to notice your breathing. Sense the flow of your breath and the rise and fall of your stomach.
- When your mind wanders to unwelcome thoughts, gently bring it back to your breath.

- Notice what you are doing as you are doing it and tune in to your senses.
- Try walking around the house (not at work!) barefoot. Concentrate on how your weight shifts and the textures of the different floor surfaces beneath your feet. Focus less on where you are headed.
- Don't feel that you need to fill up all your time with doing. Take some time to simply be.
- Take activities that you routinely carry out with little thought (such as having a bath or shower, cleaning your teeth or getting dressed). Practise carrying out these activities with more awareness of what your senses are telling you.
- Practise your empathy and compassion for others.

Leadership interview

Steve Munby – Chief Executive CfBT Education Trust

Background

Steve started his career as a secondary school teacher in Birmingham, later moving to the North East of England where he worked as a teacher and then as a lecturer. In 1987, he became a consultant on student assessment and records of achievement, working for the nine LEAs in north-east England, before becoming an inspector within the Oldham Education Department. He then went on to manage the Advisory Service in Oldham before moving to Blackburn in 1997 as the area's Assistant Director of Education. From 2000 to March 2005, he was Director of Education and Lifelong Learning in Knowsley, Merseyside. In 2005, Steve was appointed as Chief Executive of The National College of School Leadership where he stayed for seven years.

Steve is currently Chief Executive of CfBT, an international, charitable organisation with a strong reputation for working in the field of education both in the UK and globally.

The Impact of stress within the profession

Steve feels that work-related stress amongst education professionals has been a problem for some time and is probably becoming more of an issue and on the increase. He sees it as a barrier to school improvement at a national level in a range of ways.

'It is not clear-cut in every respect because in some cases, people have gone into teaching for the wrong reasons and it is not the profession for them. For those people, the fact they are feeling stressed is actually the right reaction and they need to get out.'

'Some people in the old days would have just carried on, having been teachers for most of their lives but not having been happy, but they would not have experienced the levels of accountability and pressure that they would now be under. They should have left teaching but didn't. For other's it is that they no longer have what it takes to perform well even with support.'

'Just because you are feeling stressed and under pressure, it does not mean that that is necessarily the profession or the organisation's fault,

sometimes it may be that you are in the wrong job and you need to find something that will suit you better.'

However, Steve does believe that work-related stress in teaching is creating a recruitment challenge.

'It doesn't attract the best people into the profession if they know people there who are stressed and struggling.'

'It also means that people who are already in the job may not be recommending it to others because they are finding it too hard. If people outside of teaching see their friends and peers working very long hours and looking tired and stressed, this is also not the best advertisement for the profession.'

Recruitment aside, Steve also thinks that high levels of stress impact negatively on performance.

'When staff are over-stressed they don't perform well which is bad for the children and bad for the school, but equally, when they are under-stressed they don't perform well either. Some stress is appropriate. The big issue for leadership and management in schools is to get people to the point where they are working at their best, but not over-stressed.

It is definitely not just about the length of hours you work. It is about how valued you feel and whether or not you are given new challenges along with the support to help you achieve them.'

'It is not so much about having a written policy as a matter of culture. It is certainly not about a culture of not having to work hard, or being soft on people. It is also not about a toleration of poor performance or incompetence. It is about developing a culture where there is a sense of fun, of being part of something where there is a sense of positive feedback and of being valued. Even if you are working long hours, if you feel good about what you are doing and your value is recognised you get all sorts of positive benefits from being a part of this sort of team and feeling that you are making a difference.'

'It is very much down to the culture that the leadership and management of the school create for good or ill. If it's a bullying culture, a macho culture, if it's a high accountability but low trust culture, then you will get stress in the workplace.

If you are supported, encouraged, given models of good practice to work with and given some levels of autonomy to work within; if there is fun, laughter and inclusivity within the organisation combined with a sense of achievement, then that is the secret to managing the work–life balance issue.'

Steve reports that many years ago he was once appointed to a senior position that he struggled with. It was a big step up and he was getting very stressed by it.

> 'I offered my resignation to my boss and he could have said "yes" to that and he could have got rid of a problem because I was not performing well. Instead he said, "Resignation not accepted" and he put in support for me. I ended up being very good at that job. That is the kind of difference I am talking about.'

What needs to be done at a national level?

> 'It is partly about the professional development that is offered to school leaders and potential school leaders through programmes such as the National Professional Qualification for Headship. As part of this work, we need to cover creating a culture of resilience and managing stress in the workplace.'

Steve also believes that the modelling of leadership by senior figures in education is critical. Key figures, such as the Secretary of State for Education, need to be supportive as well as challenging, building up trusting relationships.

> 'If the role models that we see at a very senior level in education are all high accountability but low trust in their approach, that will not send a powerful message to the system. If, however the models that we see make relationships important, recognise the need for humanity in leadership, and understand that everybody is fighting a battle, then that helps to create a very different kind of culture within the system.'

Personal coping strategies

> 'I have been leading organisations for nearly 15 years now and they are not without their pressures and stresses. I often find it hard to sleep.'

In terms of coping strategies:

- Firstly, I have learned to recognise signs of stress within myself so that I can take action early rather than waiting until it is much worse.
- Secondly, throughout my leadership roles I have always surrounded myself with mentors and that has been a source of great help to me.
- Thirdly, I have good support from family and friends, which is really important in a job that can be lonely.
- Fourthly, I have always believed that it is okay to admit when you are not coping, struggling or not getting things right because that makes you an authentic leader. As a leader, your colleagues will forgive you if you say that you are struggling with something or that you are not very good at something, or that you have made a mistake. What they will not forgive you for is cover-up or a blame culture. There is something good in admitting your vulnerability, that you are not the perfect leader and that you do sometime struggle and make mistakes. It is in fact a strength, and it means that you don't have to permanently bottle things up and pretend everything is okay. It is part of my leadership style to ask for help both from within the organisation and externally.
- Finally, I find that running and other forms of exercise provide me with reflection time and help to destress me.'

Managing stress in others

Steve says that, in his experience it is often easy to identify staff who are suffering stress, as many (but not all) exhibit outward signs in their face, body language and behaviour.

> 'They often look very tired or become uncharacteristically emotional or irritable. You need to talk to them about it, acknowledge it and ask what you can do to help. You then talk about support, prioritisation and not trying to do everything at once. These are the usual processes you work your way through.'

It is actually quite unusual for someone to go all the way through their professional life and not have quite significant stress. So you need to see these kinds of discussions as the norm and not the exception. You need to acknowledge that you have experienced periods of stress too.

When I was very stressed some years ago, I was unable to sleep and was exhausted. Seeing that I was in a bad way, my boss told me that I was to go home and take a few days off. It was a great thing. I wanted permission to sleep, rest, recharge my batteries and not feel I was in charge of everything for a while. To be able to do something like that without it being seen as a criticism or an admission of failure was so important to me.

The problem comes if you have given someone the support, given them time, taken away some of their responsibilities, you show humanity, kindness and understanding and things still do not get any better. That's when it gets hard. It is often not to do with work specifically, but things outside that are having an impact on work.

I don't think you should lead a slow-paced, comfortable organisation where people don't feel any stress. In the end, that does no service to the children, to the school, or the staff themselves. Children only get one chance at an education so you have to make sure that what is being delivered is the best for them. I believe in a fast-paced, hard-working, focused, energetic organisation. In addition to that, rather than instead of, it needs to be engaging and inclusive. It has to have love as well as power in its culture. It has to have humanity, kindness and compassion. It needs a sense of belonging, of being valued, of being listened to and understood.'

Summary: Chapter 9

- Optimism is an important quality in successful school leaders.
- Sometimes we need to reset our mental filters to ensure the positives are not passing us by.
- Plan more – break your to do lists down into 'must', 'should' and 'could'.
- Quick wins help us feel we are making progress towards big goals.
- List your unplanned achievements of the day.
- Music can help you to establish the feelings that you want to be feeling.
- Keep perspective by being outward-looking.
- Nobody is in charge of your happiness except you.
- The choice to be positive is a personal one.

10 Beyond the personal – Managing stress in others

We don't see things as they are, we see them as we are.

Anaïs Nin

Deepening our understanding of the nature of stress and resilience certainly allows us to manage ourselves more effectively, but also allows us greater insights into the thinking and behaviours of the people we lead. In researching this book, I have yet to meet an experienced school leader who has not had to manage a situation with a member of staff experiencing high stress levels that are impacting on their mental and emotional well-being.

Whilst the content of the book has primarily focussed on work-related stress, it would be simplistic to suggest that situations in a member of staff's personal life do not impact on their world of work. Equally, high levels of stress at work will almost certainly have an impact on home life.

As a school leader, there is generally very little you can do to change an individual's domestic stress that can be caused by so many factors, such as a relationship break-up or a bereavement. So, on the assumption that you want to help, you are confined to controlling the controllable and looking at strategies to support the individual in school.

Why would you want to help? There are four good reasons:

1 During these times of such a rapidly changing educational landscape, schools need more than ever to be resilient organisations in order to deliver the very best outcomes for the children they serve. There is much truth in the adage that the chain is only as strong as its weakest link.

2 Stress in schools can be contagious and history teaches us that panic spreads like wildfire. It needs addressing.

3 On a practical level, losing good teachers from the profession is wasteful in terms of the financial resource invested in their initial training and continuing professional development. With difficulties in recruitment to leadership roles in particular, it can pose a significant headache to individual schools in the short term and to the profession as a whole in the longer term.

4 There is, I believe, a moral imperative to care for the people we lead, otherwise we risk dehumanising them and them becoming simple tools of value only for the function they perform. Ex–service personnel who talk fondly of their commanding officers do so not just because they are great strategists, but because they care about the personnel under their command. Education is a caring profession and most school leaders are deeply empathetic, not only to the needs of their pupils, but also to their staff.

As with any medical condition, early identification is key. We must not assume that the member of staff will necessarily have recognised the signs and symptoms themselves. My own story clearly illustrates this. There was no defining moment; no switch that was flicked from 'non-stressed' to 'stressed'. Rather, it was by attrition – a gradual wearing away of my resilience until I lost all objectivity.

So if an individual cannot necessarily see the signs and symptoms themselves, what should we be looking out for?

If you remember back to chapter 1 (pages 12–13), Chris told me the classic indicators are:

Sleep, appetite, mood, concentration, tolerance and libido

Now clearly, unless you are following staff rather more closely than might professionally be considered wise(!), some of these indicators are likely to be unknowns to you, so you have rather less to work with than when you are assessing your own stress levels.

However, early indicators within a work environment may well include some or all of the following.

Challenge

If you are concerned that a member of your staff may be suffering from stress, go through this checklist marking any of the boxes that apply.

Early indicators of stress in staff: a ten-point checklist

1 **Increased absence from work** ☐

2 **Poor timekeeping** ☐
   (e.g. arriving late at the start of day or for meetings and often early to leave at the end of the day)

3 **Failure to complete tasks on time** ☐
   (e.g. not handing in their planning on time and marking not up-to-date)

4 **Rushing everywhere** ☐

5 **Unwillingness to accept feedback or advice** ☐

6 **Resistant to change**

7 **Inability to reach decisions or delegate tasks**
   (where appropriate) ☐

8 **Becoming withdrawn** ☐
   (e.g. eating lunch on their own and not interacting with close colleagues)

9 **Tearfulness** ☐

10 **Irritability with pupils or colleagues** ☐

We can all display these behaviours at times, and some of us will be more predisposed to behave in these ways, and so the key is to be looking out for *uncharacteristic behaviour* or *changes of behaviour over time*.

Having identified that a member of staff might be struggling, the next big step is deciding what to try and do about it. This takes a high degree of emotional intelligence and more than a little experience of life.

When I was at university studying to be a teacher, I served two terms on the Student Union Executive. My first position was as Entertainments Officer, organising the May ball, discos, gigs and such like. (My single best claim to fame is that I once roadied for Katrina and the Waves during the *Walking on Sunshine* era – they were desperate for help!) I really enjoyed my time as Entertainments Officer as it played to my strengths and interests. After a year's gap, I decided to stand again only this time for the post of Welfare Officer (it had just been rebranded from 'Internal Officer' which sounded suspiciously medical).

My responsibilities broadly included dealing with accommodation issues and supporting students experiencing emotional difficulties. In practice, the accommodation issues tended to be second year students and the emotional welfare issues with the first years: a range of homesick students thinking of giving up their course; break-ups of pre-university relationships; eating disorders and even a couple of students who said they were contemplating suicide.

I know that thirty years on, university pastoral systems are far more sophisticated, but back then I was woefully unsuited to be the person that other students turned to for support. Whilst very earnest and well-intentioned, I had no training and little more experience of life than the students I was trying to support. I felt the need to find a solution to every single problem put before me, and the truth of the matter was that I could not.

The reality is that for many of our staff, however much we may want to, we are not going to be able to give them their answers. Those answers have to come from within.

So what can you do to support them?

The first tier of support we can offer is to actively listen. Many of the school leaders I have interviewed have emphasised the need to establish good quality relationships where staff do actually feel that they *can* knock on your door and talk to you. As Chris Roome once told me, 'Without mutual respect – you are on a hiding to nothing!'

Others too, have emphasised the need to create *quality time* to really listen, listen and listen some more. However busy you might be, you need to create that quality time, preferably that day, in order to make them realise how important their well-being is to you.

People do not expect you to have all the answers.

What they are looking for is to limit their sense of isolation. They are looking for solidarity. Facing a situation alone can be frightening. Feeling that you are facing it with others, much less so.

When I was studying drama at university, I played the title (and only role) in Samuel Beckett's *Krapp's Last Tape*. It was the first and only time I had to carry a play completely on my own and it was a far more intimidating experience than playing as part of an ensemble. We are a social species and need supporters around us.

- **Try to get them to talk about how they are feeling:** use open-ended questions, e.g. 'You are clearly upset, do you want to talk to me about it?'
- **Don't contradict what they are thinking:** 'I know you think that but you've got it wrong!' Their feelings will be very real to them.
- **Empathise, but avoid telling someone 'you know exactly how they feel':** you will mean well, but the reality is that everyone's stress is as individual as their thumb print. Nobody knows exactly how someone else is feeling.
- **Avoid telling them that it is all going to be ok**: you don't know this and building false expectations can be more unhelpful in the long run.
- **Only agree to do something if you know you can deliver:** saying that you will do something and then not doing it is far more damaging than doing nothing at all.
- **Reflect back what they are saying to you**: e.g. 'So what you are saying is. . .' or, 'That is really causing you a lot of upset isn't it?'
- **Don't tell them what they should do**: rather, suggest things they might want to consider, e.g. 'Have you thought about talking to _____ about this?' or 'Do you think it would be worth considering going to see your GP and talking this through with him or her?'

- **Be prepared for the possibility that they may want to talk to someone completely removed from the situation – be able to signpost them to other support:** with the reduction of influence and capacity of local authorities this is less easy as many had designated Staff Welfare Officers. Our LEA Welfare Officer provided excellent support to me, visiting me at home and helping plan my phased return in 2007. It was far more helpful to me than the visits to Occupational Health. These often felt as if you were being moved through a process, rather like moving along a conveyor belt, which you would eventually drop off the end of. Many people tend to think of contacting their union if they need legal support, but actually many are able to offer support, advice, coaching and counselling through the **Education Support Partnership.**

Education Support Partnership provide a free telephone support line for all education staff across the UK. The support line is available 24 hours a day.

UK 08000 562 561
Text: 07909 341229.

www.educationsupportpartnership.org.uk

Local GP surgeries can also usually advise on what local support services may be on offer.

A short-term solution, and an effective solution for work-related stress is often to reduce a member of staff's workload and/or increase the timescale available for them to complete tasks. Even if the primary stressor is outside of work, reducing workload and allowing people some space and some thinking time, enables them to 'regroup' and gain some perspective on their situation. You are effectively buying them time. We need to be able to see the wood through the trees.

However, it is unlikely that the school will be able to sustain such changes in the long term, so it is wise to make them time specific, e.g. 'Would it help to leave early this week?' or 'Would you like me to cover your playground duties for the next couple of weeks?' or even, 'Do you need a couple of days away to think things through?'

If you have a member of staff who you think may be suffering from stress, consider:

What could you do to open a dialogue with them?

-

-

-

What, realistically, could you do to 'buy them time and thinking space'? What timescales would you attach?

-

-

-

However, Chris cautions against being overkind:

'People can easily become paranoid about the help you offer as their manager. "You are offering to take my class next lesson?" can easily be received as: "You do not think I am fit to teach next lesson!"'

'When we are under pressure, tired and anxious, we can overanalyse people's motives. Sometimes the best thing to do is simply to give somebody space.'

Chris also points out that yoga as well as many alternative therapies such as hypnosis, reflexology and acupuncture have relaxation as a core purpose. Indeed, it seems that one of the secrets of longevity, in an increasingly pressurised profession, is the ability to relax.

So far, we have looked at some of the strategies you can use to manage the situation when a member of staff *is already* suffering from stress, but what about preventative measures?

During my research, I interviewed a number of education professionals who were away from work or had recently left because of the stresses of work, in order to understand their feelings and perception of their situation.

There are two common strands that weave through their personal stories: **feeling valued** and **feeling in control.**

Feeling valued

Many of those I interviewed felt marginalised and that their face 'no longer fitted' in the school. Sometimes this was as a result of changes in leadership. This brings me back to think again about Bilbo Baggins in JRR Tolkien's *The Hobbit*. Bilbo, the most un-adventurous of creatures, was tempted to leave his comfortable home partly because he could buy into the vision but also because he saw a clear role for himself. He was needed and valued by 'the team'.

One of my failings as a head was that I was not as good as I should have been at telling people that I appreciated what they did. Internally, I did very much value the hard work I saw as I walked around the school, such as colourful and dramatic new displays of children's work, but often it was not an opportune moment to say, 'Thank you for all your hard work and producing such a colourful display'. The member of staff responsible may not have been there when I saw it or perhaps they were in full flow talking to the children. The moment would often then be lost. I would move on to the next classroom or the next building and in the busyness of the day I simply would not get back round there. As I say, this was a failing because making people feel valued and appreciated is so important in terms of their personal resilience. *What matters is perception.* Maybe I did internally value the things that I saw as I walked around the school, but if I failed to communicate that clearly then *the perception* of the staff would be that I did not. When leading whole school assemblies, I had to enunciate my words far more clearly and project my voice far more than in normal conversation. So it is with showing your appreciation of people. You almost have to overdo it in order to make sure the message gets home.

John Rees, manager of PSHE Solutions, suggests the following exercise:

Challenge

Write a list of ten things that cost no more than a pound, that will let a member of staff know that you appreciate them.

1

2

3

4

5

6

7

8

9

10

Feeling in control

Many people who are suffering from stress, anxiety or depression feel that they lack control over their professional or home lives (or both). One factor that certainly exacerbates that feeling is a perceived lack of clarity of expectations from leaders and managers (in just the same way that a lack of clarity of expectation and direction from the government or Ofsted causes stress to school leaders). Wherever possible, avoid shifting deadlines such as for submission of planning or reports (particularly forwards!) as this is likely to destabilise someone whose stress levels lie in the balance and compound the feelings of someone already feeling that they lack control.

Increasingly in schools we are seeing a tendency to homogenise systems and teaching techniques. This is understandable, particularly when schools get themselves into difficulties with Ofsted.

I recently met with a teacher, Anna, who was absent from school suffering from anxiety and depression. She had been a teacher for a number of years and had been identified as an outstanding teacher in previous Ofsted inspections. Anna tells me that she had always managed to achieve good levels of progress, but the school had, overall, received a less favourable report in its last inspection and with a new SLT in place, there was a move to bring teaching and learning styles more in line.

Anna described feeling like a left-handed child being forced to write with their right hand. 'Why do it if the handwriting is neat and legible?'

Anna felt that levels of accountability within the school were higher than they had ever been and yet she felt she had very little autonomy in terms of how she taught. Feeling marginalised and unappreciated, Anna spent less time engaging with other staff to the point that her comfort zone contracted to just being in the classroom with the children. With increased monitoring throughout the school, that zone contracted too and Anna eventually was off work for a number of weeks.

Few people would argue against the idea that schools should be accountable to the communities they serve, but getting the balance right between accountability and autonomy is crucial to the education of the pupils on the one hand and the well-being of the staff on the other.

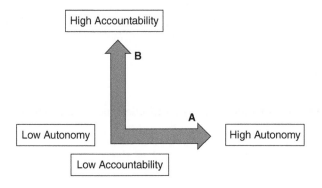

A school with low accountability and high autonomy (position A on the diagram above) would be reminiscent of the education system I joined in 1986 with no National Curriculum, no inspections, minimal monitoring of teaching and learning and teachers largely free to spend time on the subjects they enjoyed the most. There was little pressure and little incentive to develop and improve.

However, a school with very high levels of accountability but very low levels of autonomy (position B) is likely to be quite a toxic environment where targets are seen as being unattainable and, with little or no control over methodology, staff either become disengaged or stressed. We run the risk of staff becoming immobilised by the stress and anxiety they feel, rather than feeling inspired to act in the way that we may have hoped.

Of course some conformity of approach is needed in schools, but wise leaders will give staff freedoms where they can, e.g. a choice of where they take their planning, preparation and assessment time, and the ability to attend their own children's sports day. It is the cumulative effect of these small freedoms that allow an individual member of staff to feel a sense of autonomy and control. (Reminding people of these freedoms from time to time is no bad strategy, because after a time they can be taken for granted!)

Challenge

List three freedoms that staff in your school *are* currently given.

-

-

-

-

List three more that *could* be given with little or no detriment to the school.

-

-

-

Historically, the mentoring of staff in school was seen as a process for newly qualified teachers, or as a reactive measure for a member of staff who is struggling. Surely, proactive mentoring of all staff (that is not linked to pay progression!) as part of an agreed well-being policy, would help to reduce stress levels in the workplace as well as reducing the number of staff leaving the profession.

I am delighted that the NAHT are campaigning for the mentoring of all new headteachers. This would be a great step forward.

The Education Support Partnership *Education Staff Health Survey 2014* report stated that:

Just 8% said they have a well-being policy that is actually implemented.'

Given that members of staff are a schools' most important resource, it is perhaps surprising that so few schools seem to have an agreed approach or policy on staff well-being.

Challenge

If you were to develop a well-being policy for your school, what would the core principle be?

What might a policy on staff well-being look like?

Hertfordshire Schools' HR Advisory Team issued a document called *Guidance for the Management of Work Related Stress* in June 2015.

It makes clear that a duty of care for an employee's mental health is actually a legal requirement. In relation to the legal case of Walker v Northumberland County Council from 1995, the guidance draws schools' attention to the following.

'This judgement underlined the employer's duty of care to provide safe systems of work in respect of occupational stress as well as other hazards and to take steps to protect employees from foreseeable risks to mental health.'
(Hertfordshire Schools' HR Advisory Team, 2015)

As well as making the school's legal responsibilities, the guidance provides practical resources such as an Individual Stress Assessment Form and guidance on the right kind of language to use when approaching a member of staff who may be suffering from work-related stress as in these examples.

Questions to ask	Phrases to avoid
How are you feeling at the moment?	You're clearly struggling.
I've noticed you've been late (quite) a few times recently, is everything OK?	Your timekeeping is poor; I'll be keeping my eye on things going forward.

The full policy can be found online www.thegrid.org.uk/schoolworkforce/human_resources/policies/#w

When trying to support staff suffering from stress it is very helpful to know the range of support services that are readily available.

In 2012, Wiltshire Council produced a policy, entitled: *Model Staff Well-being: Policy and Guidance for Schools and Academies.* As well as being agreed with all the main unions, this policy also includes some very clear signposting to support services.

'**Human Resources** *can provide guidance on the scope and range of options available to headteachers or governors in particular situations. This helps to ensure fair and consistent management standards, which in turn provides reassurances to staff.'*
(Wiltshire Council, 2012)

The policy goes on outline the support available from the Occupational Health Service, Health and Safety Service and trade union appointed representatives.

The appeal of 'off the shelf policies' where you can simply insert the name of your school is strong, particularly when time is tight and it means you can tick off a box. These policies are absolutely fine and certainly better than nothing at all as long as, as a school 'we walk the walk' and 'talk the talk' because like school vision statements, just because you've written one, it does not make it true. The Education Support Partnership survey (see above, page 178) does not say that 8% *have* a well-being policy, they say only 8% have one that is 'always implemented'.

> 'The results suggested that such policies are effective with individuals working in an environment where staff health and well-being was carefully monitored reporting significantly lower levels of mental health conditions: those suffering from anxiety fell by more than a third to 49%, stress dropped to 75% and depression to 31%.'
>
> (The Education Support Partnership, *Education Staff Health Survey 2014*)

Some of the best policies I have seen are personalised to the school and demonstrate a clear commitment from the governors and school leadership. They give a flavour of the school's context, what they feel is important and give practical examples of strategies they have put in place to reduce stress.

Take these extracts from Portswood & St Mary's CE Primary Schools' *Staff Well-being Policy Statement and Guidelines,* for example.

> '*Portswood & St Mary's CE Primary Schools recognise that the staff are their most important resource and are to be valued, supported and encouraged to develop personally and professionally within a learning and caring community. There is a relationship between healthier more positive staff, pupil achievement and school improvement.'*
>
> *The policy also talks about the importance of opportunities for staff to socialise and relax, appropriate induction for new staff, the quality of staff facilities, open and listening management systems that respond quickly to issues and regular monitoring of staff absence.*
>
> **'Examples of Good Practice**
> *Limits will be placed on staff time in school – the Senior Leadership Team will set the example for others to follow. All staff are expected to leave early one day a week (Friday) i.e. by 4.30pm.'*
>
> (Portswood & St Mary's CE Primary School, 2013)

One Inset day each year for report writing, time for subject and phase leaders to carry out major tasks and the provision of free weekly yoga are also features of the policy.

For reference purposes you can find the whole document at: http://www.st-marys-pri.southampton.sch.uk/wp-content/policies/Wellbeing.pdf

The very localised and personal approach to staff well-being appeals to me greatly. You really feel that staff well-being really matters and I would encourage other schools to take a similar approach.

Staff are our most important resource. Their well-being is crucial to the success of the school and the quality of education we provide for our children.

Take control...

Nutrition

Stress is a problem in itself, but sometimes when we are under stress, we tend to make poor food choices. These choices can create more stress in the long run, affecting our sleep, weight and ability to cope with the pressures of the day. This is often termed as 'emotional eating'.

The chemical changes brought about by stress responses affect people differently. Some people skip meals, sometimes unknowingly others snack and crave unhealthy foods, high in fats, sugar and salt. Excessive nervous energy can often lead people to eat more than they normally would.

Too much caffeine can lead to poor concentration, decreased effectiveness, sleep disturbances, and increased levels of cortisol in the blood.

- Make sure you start the day with breakfast – otherwise you have nothing to start up your metabolism with.
- Eat three meals a day – skipping meals means that we are more likely to pick at unhealthy foods later.
- Remember the old saying, 'Eat like a king in the morning, a prince at noon and a pauper at night'!
- Avoid using excessive caffeine to 'kick-start' your system in the morning, as it can lead to a pattern of all-day coffee drinking. High caffeine levels can make us hyperactive and anxious.
- If you currently consume a lot of coffee, try weaning yourself off it gradually.
- Remember caffeine is not only found in coffee but also tea, cocoa, drinking chocolate, chocolate and cola drinks.
- Some people find it effective to gradually substitute coffee with decaffeinated green tea, which has a soothing taste as well as having the added benefit of lots of antioxidants.
- Drink plenty of water throughout the day to keep your system hydrated and keep hunger pangs at bay.
- Limit consumption of alcohol. It can be a relaxant but increasing your consumption when stressed is likely to affect your metabolism

negatively. Alcohol may help you to drop off to sleep quickly, but frequently causes sleep disturbance.

- Avoid smoking cigarettes as they are addictive. For some, smoking removes the presence of stress in the short term, but the detrimental effects on long-term health are well documented.
- Regulate consumption of fast or convenience foods.
- Avoid crash dieting or diets that do not provide a balance nutritionally.
- If you find you need to eat between meals, avoid sweets and chocolate as they too will increase your caffeine levels. (Chris reports that a peak time of year for referrals is after Easter, when many people's chocolate intake soars.) Fruit such as blueberries and bananas (which give a slow release of energy), yoghurts, salad foods or nuts make good alternatives. Granola bars are suitable and filling too.
- Limit sugar consumption. It contains no goodness or vital nutrients that we require. Sugar also gives people a significant burst of energy for a short period of time only. When this 'high' runs out, people suffer a comedown from this and experience a lengthy 'low' period.
- We need a balance nutritionally for our body and minds to function well. These include:
    o B vitamins – which can be found in foods such as seaweed and raw foods.
    o Proteins and iron – found in meat, eggs, seeds and nuts.
    o A vitamins – found in cheese, eggs, fish with oil, and milk.
    o C vitamins – found in fruits (such as apples, bananas and oranges).
    o Magnesium – found in green leafy vegetables such as cabbage, fish, meat and dairy products.

B vitamins and magnesium are particularly important in helping the body and mind combat stress.

Leadership interview

Chris Thinnes – Educator and consultant, Los Angeles, USA

Background

Chris Thinnes is a veteran independent school leader in the United States, an active collaborator with educators from the private and public (state) sectors, and an engaged public school parent. For 15 years, Chris served in a variety of senior leadership positions at Curtis School in Los Angeles, most recently as both the Head of the Upper Elementary School and the Academic Dean – actively collaborating at the same time with education leaders, researchers, and activists from the public and private sectors to advance a shared commitment to transform teaching and learning for all the nation's children.

In the 2013–2014 school year, Chris was honoured as a Fellow of the Martin Institute for Teaching Excellence, and named one of Carney Sandoe's '8 Thought Leaders to follow now'. He is currently consulting with several independent, charter, parochial, and public schools in Los Angeles, while pursuing his Ed.D. in Education Leadership for Social Justice at Loyola Marymount University, and establishing the Center for the Future of Education & Democracy (CFED) as its Founding Executive Director.

The impact of stress within the profession

As well as the stresses brought to bear upon student learners over the last couple of decades as a result of national education policy, Chris sees work-related stress as a critical issue within the teaching profession within the United States and there are real issues around recruitment and retention of teachers.

'It is to some degree, an unexplored issue due to everybody's prevailing concerns over pedagogy and policy. There is more of a dialogue opening up in independent schools around concepts of work–life balance, mindfulness practice and efficacy of one's practice. I'm not sure sometimes whether the conversation is more about holistic health or ways to make saner employees more productive, but none-the-less the debate is opening up. However, independent schools represent such a small proportion of schools in the American education sector that I don't know how influential that practice will become. I have an inclination that people might see it as a 'fru-fru' add-on of a privileged independent

school experience rather than a necessary core commitment of education practice.'

'For me it is less about the logistical concerns of day to day leadership practice and more about the philosophical constructs of what good leadership looks like. Most schools are still caught up in the idea of hierarchical leadership where most, if not all responsibilty for institutional decision-making rests with an authoritarian head of school, principal, or district leader. Balance comes from more distributed leadership and more democratic forms of governance, which is slowly taking root in some schools. In my own experience, the more that I involved other people in developing a shared vision and a mutual ownership of change initiatives, the less I felt like a lunatic that was falling apart at the seams. That's not why I did it, but it was certainly a consequence.'

'The other thing is that we know so much about what children actually need, but we have difficulty putting it into practice and that leads to a deep sense of frustration and stress. There is real urgency of transforming our schools to what they need to be at every level but a real sense of difficulty in making the necessary changes in anything but the most incremental ways. There is huge frustration in continually fighting for a goal and not seeing the transformative impact in the way that one might like.'

Chris is convinced that these frustrations and stresses are having a significant impact on the national school improvement agenda.

'Thinking more here, about the public education sector rather than the independent, the role of the teacher has been redefined and the idea of teaching as transmission has been entrenched again, through high stakes testing and accountability policies, the Common Core standards movement, and other policies. It has removed for many teachers the sense of autonomy, agency and craftsmanship that many people consider a vital part of the profession. Teachers feel less invested than ever with the authority to make key decisions about how to help children, and that stripping of agency is at the root of much of the stress that American teachers are feeling. Many professionals understand that what they are being asked to do is at odds with what they know is good for children. They understand too the very real consequences of defying policy mandates and so they end up doing things on a daily basis that

they know are at odds with the very reasons that they became teachers in the first place. I have seen this in teachers I have worked with and teachers who have taught my son. It also seems the common pattern in much of anecdotal and empirical research about what is happening in American schools. You can look at the notions of agency, autonomy and professional efficacy as a philosophical abstraction but there is a great deal of research that ties these notions directly back to anxiety and dispassion. This is causal, in my opinion, to low retention rates amongst teachers and a great number leaving the profession entirely.'

What needs to be done at a national level?

Chris is clear that the public perception of the profession in America is a significant factor in the high number of teachers leaving the profession.

'People easily turn to business models for new language and new ideas about how to think of teaching and learning, and yet it would be unthinkable for reformers in medicine to turn to say legal practice or accountancy for their inspiration and language. It is as though there is a shared belief that there is no fount of professional wisdom, no research base and no decades and decades of past practice to draw upon from within the education profession itself.'

'We need to look at how American teachers are paid and how they are viewed in popular culture. The feeling that the profession is highly disrespected and that 'every day is a proving day' is the root cause of so much of the stress. Moving from a deficit-based view of American teaching and moving to affirmative enquiry into what can, does and always does work, would be a philosophical shift that I would love to see. I actually think that this is a global phenomenon.'

One of Chris's favourite quotes that has helped him through the years comes from the mentor of Robert Reich, former Labour Secretary in President Clinton's administration:

'Don't confuse the difficulty of attaining a goal with the urgency of fighting for it.' (Robert Reich)

Personal coping strategies

On a philosophical level:

- Being willing to acknowledge that I don't know something when I don't. That gives me tremendous freedom as opposed to a traditional construct of having to be an expert in everything. I acknowledge the limitations of my own knowledge and skills set

- Listening to understand rather than to respond. I am thinking here of the stress in dealing with difficult situations with teachers or parents, where my instinct is to brace myself for conflict. If you listen to understand the conversation becomes a different experience. It diminishes my stress and improves my understanding.
- Distributive leadership. I know the limits of my own capacity to pretend to be responsible for everything and invite a community into shared responsibility. Leadership is an opportunity to facilitate, support and catalyze a shared vision rather than an obligation to construct or prescribe it on my own.

On a practical level:

'Taking regular breaks. I discovered some years ago that I needed to take a series of five-minute walks by myself during the course of the day. I have found that to be more sustaining than one longer break.'

'Developing ally ships both within the school gates and outside it. I have always made sure that I have at least one person in the school I can 'shut the door' with and dump whatever was in our craws. It is not necessarily about finding a solution – it's cathartic. I also always had a leader in another school who had no understanding of the local context, but we could always call one another. They were mutually understood as safe and fair relationships. Those conversations were never viewed as an imposition or an interruption.'

Managing stress in others

It is sometimes hard to separate policy from reality and Chris recognises that a lot of public schools have very little latitude or flexibility. However, he maintains that something that schools can do is strive to reduce teachers' sense of isolation.

'With enormous class sizes (often 40–50 students) throughout the day and an inconceivable workload, more and more teachers have fewer and fewer opportunities to collaborate at any level, denying them the opportunity to exist in community with other teachers and leaving them feeling very isolated and creating stress. Changing the boundaries of what is appropriate professional dialogue can help, and finding those opportunities for collaboration where they exist. Reducing isolation is critical.'

One of Chris's strategies to help other people to manage their own stress was to develop a common understanding around deadlines for a shared responsibility such as the completion of a curriculum plan or report cards.

'These deadlines were artificial constructs. We all have life circumstances that sometimes mean that we cannot meet a deadline and whilst our professional obligations are very important, particularly when they impact on others, for people to know that there is some flexibility on deadlines, if needed, makes a huge difference to people.'

Chris has had seven major back operations and ensuing periods of recovery. There have been times when he has been at work when he shouldn't have been, but needed to be.

'It's a powerful experience to be given, by colleagues, the space to get through.'

As such, he appreciates that other staff too can have life situations that can prevent them from working at their full capacity at times and has been able to give them that space too, when needed.

'It's about building a shared community where people are willing to volunteer to fill for someone for a short while, or cover their responsibilities. You need to build a community rooted in shared goals, collective responsibility and empathy for your colleagues' needs.'

Summary: Chapter 10

- Resilient schools need resilient staff.
- Proactive mentoring of staff can aid early identification of stress.
- Establishing positive relationships based on mutual respect is crucial.
- Effective leaders make opportunities for quality time to listen.
- People's solutions often lie within themselves. Showing solidarity and buying them thinking time can be an effective strategy.
- Feeling valued and having a sense of personal autonomy are vital to maintaining personal resilience levels.
- Schools need a proactive, agreed approach to the well-being of their most important resource; the staff.

Conclusion

I recently returned to Bradgate Park, in Leicestershire, scene of so many childhood walks. I climbed all the way to the top of one of the tallest hills and stood next to 'Old John', the stone folly that is visible from miles around. With height and distance, I could see where all the very many pathways that criss-cross the park interconnected. This clarity is hard to obtain when you are further down the park and stand amongst the thick bracken that can obscure your vision, leaving you uncertain of where the paths lead and how they all connect up.

Time and distance has also given me perspective on the events of a few years ago and I am able to talk about it in a way that I could not have done before: it was too raw. I am able to look back and review what happened to me with greater clarity and objectivity. It has been, in many ways a cathartic experience, and I have developed a real interest in understanding the patterns of my thinking and behaviour that both hindered me and then later helped me recover. Working with Chris Roome on this book and understanding what he was thinking and trying to do to help me during my treatment, has been particularly enlightening. It has at times felt like a somewhat 'out of body experience' hovering above oneself and observing.

My stress and break down of resilience was caused by a combination of the pressures of my job and my own mindset. Each affected the other, but I have to take personal responsibility for the latter. We always have choices in how we behave and react to situations and stressors.

There are many things that I would do differently with the benefit of hindsight (which is of course a wonderful thing), but amongst the most significant lessons I have learned are these:

- Firstly, listen to what your body is telling you. A bad back, migraines, panic attacks and even a stammer on their own may not be an indicator, but when lots of warning lights come up on your dashboard at once, it is time to pull over and check out what is wrong.
- We all need to challenge ourselves to step outside our comfort zone. If we do, our comfort zone expands. If we don't, our comfort zone does not stay the same size, it rapidly shrinks.

- Isolation is the worst enemy of resilience. Without support to affirm our positive self-beliefs and challenge our negative ones, we run the risk of losing all perspective. Build alliances and find mentors.
- It is not a weakness to ask for help and assistance. Nor is there any shame in doing so. It is actually a trait of effective school leaders and a key factor in maintaining resilience over time.
- In short, we need to draw people in, not push them away.
- We cannot expect other colleagues to display these characteristics if we are not modelling them ourselves. Over time, as David Taylor says, 'Your personality, becomes their personality'. (*The Naked Leader*).
- Much of my isolation in 2006 and 2007 was self-imposed. I thought that I was the only one struggling to cope with some of the stresses and strains of the job – nobody else seemed to admit to it and I felt embarrassed and ashamed that I was. Ironically, cutting myself from other people only served to perpetuate that myth.

Travelling around the country, speaking about my experiences at conferences and running workshops on stress management techniques, I have been deeply touched by the positive feedback I have received and the number of people who have felt able to come over at the end of sessions and share their own experiences on the vital, but largely not talked about issue of stress.

I have come to realise that I was not on my own back then. There are many people battling with their personal stress levels at work. I am tremendously grateful to all those leaders of education who have shared so openly their experiences and offered their advice through the interviews in this book. The common thread that runs throughout, is that we become stressed by those factors that are beyond our control and influence.

Whilst resilience levels vary from individual to individual, no one should make the mistake of thinking that they are immune from a potential and severe reaction to stress.

This is not just about me and it is not only a national issue, it is an international one. I was talking recently with a young German teacher who was visiting England, and she asked what I was writing a book about. When I told her it was about educational leadership, stress and resilience she told me that it was a significant issue in Germany too. Only five out of thirty of the schools in their local cluster currently have substantive headteachers due to the difficulties in recruiting to an increasingly pressurised role.

Chris Thinnes's summary of the situation in the US (pages 190–194) closely parallels the mistrust of the profession by some politicians in this country and the lack of respect for the contribution of those that work with children day in, day out, in national policy making.

Children only get one chance at an education and schools should be ambitious and accountable. They should also be places built on the values of trust, humanity and compassion.

Steve Munby has said that where there is a culture of high accountability and low trust, you will always get stress (page 169).

I don't know anyone left in the profession who does not think that schools should not be accountable. That is not the real source of stress. The stress comes from a feeling of powerlessness and trying to respond to raft after raft of policy changes and shifting expectations borne out of a lack of trust.

This lack of trust does not come from the general public. Indeed a recent Ipsos MORI poll showed teachers to be regarded as the second most trusted profession in Great Britain (86% trust rating) second only to doctors (90%). Politicians fared rather less well!

The perceived lack of trust comes rather from those politicians who have little experience or no experience in teaching but draw upon personal idealogy, rather than the fount of knowledge of how children learn best that lies within the profession, to impose a system of education in their own image. This creates in itself daily tensions for professionals who have to balance what they are expected to do with what they believe is actually best for their pupils.

Until we address the issue of stress and create a culture of high accountability and high levels of trust throughout the education system, we will not recruit and retain the calibre of staff that our schools need and our young people deserve. That culture needs to be modelled from the very top.

We need to ensure that we treat adults and professionals with the same sensitivity and duty of care that we afford to our children. As people, young or old, we possess fundamental rights and basic needs in order to thrive. This is as true of mental health as it is of physical health. To that end, we need to feel valued, connected and trusted; we need control over our lives and that we will be supported if we need help.

In return for all this, we need to behave with the honesty and openness we see in our children. We need to have the confidence to learn, make mistakes and to be able to laugh.

My leadership story is one of hope and optimism. If you had told me in 2007, when I was at my lowest ebb and could barely get out a sentence, that I would one day give the opening keynote at the NAHT annual conference, or appear on television, I would have thought you were mad. If you told me that one day I would be a published author sharing my experiences, I would have laughed. But, you see, no problem is insurmountable if you have the right mindset and the tools to cope.

I am far more self-aware than I have ever been before. I don't so much feel that I have arrived at a destination, but that I am still *en route*, much happier in my own skin and learning all the time. There is no magic wand to be waved and I recognise that the potential for stress will always be in me at some level, but I now have the confidence, strategies and support to control it.

Ironically, I am back to doing what I always did best – teaching. The audience and the medium may be different, but the opportunity to share experiences and help others to make sense of the world remains the greatest privilege of all.

Appendix

Summary of leadership interviews findings

In the course of writing this book, I have interviewed a number of headteachers and leaders of education. As well as contributing significantly to the advice offered in Chapter 7 on handling the pressure of an Ofsted inspection, I generally asked them four main questions:

1 What causes you the most stress in your role?
2 What coping strategies do you use to manage your stress?
3 How do you manage stress in the people you lead?
4 What advice would you offer to someone new to headship or any other senior leadership position?

Below, is a summary of their most common responses.

What causes you the most stress in your role?

The most common response was the accountabilities around an Ofsted inspection. For most, it was not the inspection itself, but often the potential, and very public attention should a school lose its 'Outstanding' grading, or drop from 'Good' to 'Requires improvement'. There were also frustrations around the 'moving of goalposts' of the expectations that must be met in order to achieve or retain each grading.

A second, very common source of stress, was trying to resolve ongoing staffing issues and, in particular, staff absence. Unpredictability and having to settle for cover solutions that are less than ideal were cited as being particular pressures, along with only being able to divulge very limited information to parents who, understandably, want to see any disruption to their child's education minimised.

Handling issues with parents was another common theme. For most, it was not so much the quantity of such issues as the unpredictability of them. Resolving matters with unhappy or concerned parents can also be costly, taking heads away from other equally important but planned tasks during the day.

The fourth most common source of stress was the frequency of change in government policy. It was the pace of change, rather than change itself, that brings so much pressure.

What coping strategies do you use to manage your stress?

The leaders that I interviewed recognised the need to be able to relax and find strategies that take the mind as well as the body away from school.

Most saw exercise as an effective way of unwinding, be it walking the dog, dance classes or regularly visiting the gym.

Other forms of relaxation included reading books, watching films, vacations and time spent with family and friends.

The need to have people to offload to and talk things through with was identified as being very important, both within the work context itself, but also amongst family and friends.

Retaining a sense of humour was seen as being important, along with the ability to remind yourself of your moral purpose – why we do the job.

How do you manage stress in the people you lead?

A recurring theme here was that headteachers need to invest time into building relationships with their staff to gain trust and respect. They need to be seen to be available and take time to really listen.

Heads need to role model the behaviours that they want to see in their staff.

Honesty and clarity of expectations were seen as important. Pressure is part of the job but needs to be at an appropriate level. Routinely sheltering people from it, does not help them in the long term.

Staff need to understand the rationale behind decisions and how things piece together.

All staff need someone that they know they can go and talk to. It may not be the Head, but structures need to reflect that.

Staff need to have fun at work!

What advice would you offer to someone new to headship or any other senior leadership position?

Pacing yourself was seen to be very important. Not only in terms of managing workload but also career progression. People are going to have to work for longer and people are often promoted to leadership positions younger. It will be a marathon not a sprint. Choose jobs carefully.

Accept the limitations of your knowledge; teamwork is the way forward.

Maintaining outside interests was seen to be vital, along with the abilty to say 'no' sometimes, without feeling guilty.

Don't take yourself too seriously, keep your sense of humour.

Work to live; don't live to work.

Bibliography and recommended reading

Association of Teachers and Lecturers (April 2014), 'Pressures on teachers causing rise in mental health issues' (www.atl.org.uk/Images/11%20for%2014%20Apr%20 2014%20-%20annual%20conf%20mental%20health%20issues.pdf)

BBC (2015) Teacher stress levels in England 'soaring', data shows (www.bbc.co.uk/ news/education-31921457)

Business Matters magazine (November 2012), 'Stress costs UK economy £3.7BN' (www.bmmagazine.co.uk/news/stress-costs-uk-economy-3–7bn/)

Campbell, J. (1993) *The Hero with a Thousand Faces*, Fontana Press

Cope, A. and Whittaker, A. (2012), *The Art of Being Brilliant*, Capstone

Department for Education (2015), *Workload challenge: Analysis of teacher responses* research report (https://www.gov.uk/government/uploads/system/uploads/ attachment_data/file/401406/RR445_-_Workload_Challenge_-_Analysis_of_ teacher_consultation_responses_FINAL.pdf)

Eggert, M. (1992, new ed. 2007), *The Perfect Interview: All You Need to Get it Right First Time*, Random House

Elkin, A. (2013), *Stress Management for Dummies*, John Wiley & Sons

Findlater, S. (2015), *How to Survive an Ofsted Inspection*, Bloomsbury

Gibson, S., Oliver, L. and Dennison, M. (February 2015), *Workload Challenge: Analysis of Teacher Consultation Responses Research Report*, CooperGibson Research, DfE (www.gov.uk/government/uploads/system/uploads/attachment_data/ file/401406/RR445_-_Workload_Challenge_-_Analysis_of_teacher_consultation_ responses_FINAL.pdf)

Gilbert, I. (2004), *Little Owl's Book of Thinking: An Introduction to Thinking Skills*, Crown House Publishing

Hasson, G. (2014), *Emotional Intelligence: Managing Emotions to Make a Positive Impact on Your Life and Career*, Capstone

Health and Safety Executive, 'Definition of stress' www.hse.gov.uk/stress/ furtheradvice/whatisstress.htm

Health and Safety Executive (2014), *Stress and Psychological Disorders in Great Britain 2014* www.hse.gov.uk/statistics/causdis/stress/stress.pdf

Health and Social Care Information Centre (July 2015), *Prescriptions dispensed in the community in England 2004–14* (www.hscic.gov.uk/catalogue/PUB17644/pres- disp-com-eng-2004–14-rep.pdf)

Hertfordshire Schools' HR Advisory Team (June 2015) *Guidance for the Management of Work Related Stress* (www.thegrid.org.uk/schoolworkforce/human_resources/ policies/#w)

Houdmont et al. (2012), *Occupational Medicine*

ipsos MORI poll (January 2015) (www.ipsos-mori.com/researchpublications/
researcharchive/3504/Politicians-trusted-less-than-estate-agents-bankers-and-
journalists.aspx)

Johnstone, C. (2010), *Find Your Power*, Permanent Publications

Kennerley, H. (1997, 2009), *Overcoming Anxiety: A Self-help Guide to Using Cognitive
Behavioural Techniques,* Robinson Publishing

Lillas. C (2010), www.integrationtraining.co.uk/blog/2010/05/stress-symptoms.html

Looker, T. and Gregson, O. (1997), *Teach Yourself: Managing Stress*, Hodder &
Stoughton

Maxwell, J. C. www.johnmaxwell.com/blog/delegation-by-way-of-development

McGee, P (2015), *S.U.M.O (Shut Up, Move On): The Straight-Talking Guide to Succeeding
in Life* Capstone; 10th Anniversary Edition

Mosier, H. (2011), *Stress Less, Weigh Less: Follow Holly to Increase Energy, Eat the Food
You Love & Enjoy an Ageless Body,* Greenleaf Book Group

Newcastle, North Tyneside and Northumberland Mental Health NHS Trust (2002),
Stress: A Self-help Guide

Norris, R. (2006), *The Promised Land: A Guide to Positive Thinking for Sufferers of Stress,
Anxiety and Depression*, AuthorHouse

Peters, S. (2012), *The Chimp Paradox*, Vermillion

Portswood & St Mary's CE Primary Schools (2013), *Staff Well-being Policy Statement
and Guidelines* (www.st-marys-pri.southampton.sch.uk/wp-content/policies/
Wellbeing.pdf)

Reich R (2013), *Can there ever be economic equality in America?* (www.csmonitor.com/
Business/Robert-Reich/2013/0829/Can-there-ever-be-economic-equality-in-
America)

Richards, D. and McDonald, B. (1990), *Behavioural Psychotherapy: A Handbook for
Nurses*, Butterworth-Heinemann Ltd.

Robinson, J. W. (1980), *Helping others manage stress* (www.joe.org/joe/1980may/80-3-
a8.pdf)

Seligman, M. (1995), Learned Helplessness: A Theory for the Age of Personal Control'
Oxford University Press, U.S.A. New Ed edition (5 Oct. 1995

Society of Occupational Medicine (February 2012), 'Large new study shows recession
increases work-related stress by 40%' (www.som.org.uk/news/media-releases/
single-media/article/large-new-study-shows-recession-increases-work-related-
stress-by-40-28/)

Stress Management Society and Bodychef: 'Combating stress with a balanced
nutritional diet' (www.stress.org.uk/files/combat-nutritional-stress.pdf)

Sutcliffe, J. (2013), *8 Qualities of Successful School Leaders: The Desert Island Challenge*,
Bloomsbury

Taylor, D. (2002), *The Naked Leader*, Capstone

Bibliography and Recommended Reading

Teachers Assurance Company Ltd (May 2012), 'Teachers assurance survey'
   (www.teachersassurance.co.uk/money-news/teachers-stress-levels-affecting-
   performance)
The Education Support Partnership (previously The Teacher Support Network
   Group) (2014), *Education Staff Health Survey 2014*, Education Support Partnership
   (teachersupport.info/research-policy/research-reports/education-staff-health-
   survey-2014)
The Guardian (December 2012), 'Rise in teachers off work with stress – and union
   warns of worse to come' (www.theguardian.com/education/2012/dec/26/
   teachers-stress-unions-strike)
The Guardian (May 2015), 'Headteachers at "coasting" schools face threat of sack'
   (www.theguardian.com/education/2015/may/17/headteachers-at-coasting-
   schools-face-threat-of-sack)
Tolkien, J. R. R. (1937 1st edition; 2011), *The Hobbit*, HarperCollins
Wilshaw, M. (2012), (www.theguardian.com/education/2012/may/10/teachers-dont-
   know-stress-ofsted-chief)
Wiltshire Council (2012), *Model Staff Well-being: Policy and Guidance for Schools and
   Academies* (http://wisenet.wiltshire.gov.uk/documents/dsweb/Get/Document-
   12305/A196–12%20School%20Staff%20Well-Being%20Policy%20and%20
   Toolkits%20July%202012.doc)

Audio recordings

CD: *Ocean waves at sunset*, (2003) © New World Music
CD: *Relax with nature volume 3: Natural sounds*, (2003) © New World Music
   http://www.phrases.org.uk/meanings/darkest-hour.html

Index